Charles Pinckney James

The Power of Congress to Punish Contempts and Breaches of Privilege

Charles Pinckney James

The Power of Congress to Punish Contempts and Breaches of Privilege

ISBN/EAN: 9783337038748

Printed in Europe, USA, Canada, Australia, Japan

Cover: Foto ©Suzi / pixelio.de

More available books at **www.hansebooks.com**

THE POWER OF CONGRESS

TO PUNISH

CONTEMPTS AND BREACHES OF PRIVILEGE.

BY

CHARLES P. JAMES,

Of the Washington Bar.

WASHINGTON, D. C.:
W. H. & O. H. MORRISON.
1879.

THE POWER OF CONGRESS TO PUNISH CONTEMPTS AND BREACHES OF PRIVILEGE.

I.

A DOUBT has never ceased to exist in the minds of many lawyers, notwithstanding the decision in *Anderson* vs. *Dunn*, 6 Wheaton's Rep., 204, whether general power to adjudicate and inflict punishment for contempts and breaches of privilege, has been vested by the Constitution in the Senate and House of Representatives of the United States; and expressions of this doubt have been revived as often as any noticeable instance of its exercise has attracted attention.

It has been felt that a claim of power affecting personal liberty, which is not referred to by any word in the Constitution, but is based wholly upon an implication from necessity, stands upon grounds which are uncertain; and that it has not been rendered unquestionable even by long usage. A candid inquiry into the sufficiency of these grounds seems, therefore, not to be improper, or to come too late. It is hoped that the following discussion preserves that character. And it should be added, that such an inquiry recognizes the necessity that these offenses should be punished; it proposes nothing more than a consideration of the provisions which the Constitution has made for that purpose. It is incumbent upon any person who questions a power which assumes to be settled by authority and practice, to exhibit at the outset, as fully as possible, the argument in its behalf. Instances of its exercise showing how early they began, and the reasoning by which they have been vindicated, will therefore be now presented.

On the 28th of December, 1795, upon information given by several members in their places, of an attempt made by one Robert Randall to corrupt them, the House of Representatives directed the Speaker to issue his warrant of arrest, and on the next day Randall was taken in custody. He was detained until the 6th of January, when the House, by a vote of seventy-eight to seventeen, came to the following resolution: "That it appears to this House that Robert Randall has been guilty of a contempt to and a breach of the privileges of this House, by attempting to corrupt the integrity of its members in the manner laid to his charge." And thereupon it was resolved: "That the said Robert Randall be brought to the bar, reprimanded by the Speaker, and committed to the custody of the Sergeant-at-Arms, until the further order of this House." Pursuant to this resolution, Randall was brought to the bar, reprimanded, and remanded to the custody of the Sergeant, by whom he was detained until the 13th of January, when he was discharged by order of the House on payment of fees.

Five years later, in March, 1800, occurred the case of William Duane. A bill had been introduced in the Senate by Ross, of Pennsylvania, prescribing the mode of deciding disputed elections of President and Vice-President, of which the principal feature was the appointment by ballot of a joint committee of both houses, with power to decide absolutely on the validity of any objections to any of the electoral votes. In reference to this bill, Duane had charged in the *Aurora*, a newspaper published in Philadelphia, that it was got up by a secret caucus of Federal Senators, who controlled all the proceedings of that body, with the design to deprive Pennsylvania of her vote at the ensuing presidential election. The Senate, upon the report of a committee of privileges, to whom this publication had been referred, resolved that it contained " assertions and pretended information, respecting the Senate and their proceedings," " false, defamatory, scandalous, and malicious, tending to defame the Senate, and to bring them into contempt and disrepute, and to excite against them the hatred of the good people of the United States, and that the said publication was a high breach of the privileges of the Senate." Having appeared at the bar in obedience to a summons, Duane asked permission to be assisted by counsel, which was granted, with the limitation that they should be heard only as to such questions of *fact* as might arise, or in excuse or extenuation of his offense. Dallas and Thomas Cooper, to whom he applied, declined to act as counsel, since they were not to be allowed to dispute the constitutionality of the proceeding. Duane, claiming that he was deprived, under the restrictions which the Senate had seen fit to impose, of all professional assistance, declined any further voluntary attendance upon that body; and the Senate voted that he was guilty of contempt in refusing to appear; directing the Sergeant-at-Arms to arrest him, and to hold him in custody until further orders. Hildreth's Hist. of the U. S., Vol. 2, p. 352, 2d Series.

This proceeding of the Senate performed substantially the office of an ordinary prosecution for libel, and their formally expressed resolution had, to a remarkable degree, the ring of an indictment.

In January, 1818, another attempt to corrupt its members was brought to the attention of the House of Representatives. A member in his place informed the House that John Anderson had attempted to bribe him, with a view to influence his action on certain claims then pending there. Upon an unanimous vote the Speaker issued his warrant, Anderson was taken into custody, and was subsequently brought to their bar from time to time, as directed, until finally, on the 16th of January, the House came to the following resolution : " That John Anderson has been guilty of a contempt and a violation of the privileges of the House, and that he be brought to the bar of the House this day, and be there reprimanded by the Speaker for the outrage he has committed, and then discharged from the custody of the Sergeant-at-Arms."

On the 14th of April, 1832, the Speaker laid before the House of Representatives a communication from a member, stating that on the evening of the previous day he had been attacked, knocked down by a bludgeon, and severely bruised and wounded by Samuel Houston, for words spoken in his place in the House. Thereupon, the usual warrant was issued, and Houston was taken in custody by the Sergeant-at-Arms. On the 11th of May, it was resolved by the House : " That Samuel Houston has been guilty of a contempt and violation of the privileges of this House;" and on the same day the House passed a further resolution: "That Samuel Houston be brought to the bar of the House on Monday next, at twelve o'clock, and be there reprimanded by the Speaker for the contempt and violation of the privileges of the House of which he has been guilty, and that he be discharged from the custody of the Sergeant-at-Arms."

In March, 1848, John Nugent was summoned to appear at the bar of the Senate as a witness; and, having appeared, he was sworn, but refused to answer certain interrogatories then propounded to him. For this refusal, he was adjudged to have committed a contempt against the Senate, and was ordered into the custody of the Sergeant-at-Arms, there to remain until the further order of the Senate.

In January, 1857, J. W. Simonton was summoned as a witness before a select committee of the House of Representatives, appointed to investigate charges that members of that House had entered into corrupt combinations for the purpose of securing the passage of certain measures by Congress; and during the progress of the investigation, certain questions were propounded to him, which he declined to answer. The committee reported this fact to the House, the Speaker was ordered to issue his warrant, and Simonton was immediately brought in custody to the bar. After he had been heard in his own defense, the House passed the following resolution: "Whereas, J. W. Simonton having appeared at the bar of the House, according to its order, and the cause assigned for the said contempt being unsatisfactory, therefore—Resolved, That the said J. W. Simonton be continued in close custody by the Sergeant-at-Arms, or, in his absence, by Mr. William G. Flood, during the balance of this session, or until discharged by the further order of the House, to be taken when he shall have purged the contempt on which he was arrested, by testifying before the committee."

It is unnecessary, however, to set out all of the instances of the exercise of this power. Enough have been cited to show the kind of acts to which it has been held by the two houses of Congress to extend, and the manner of its use. It is proper, next, to state the arguments by which the power has been supported.

In *Duane's* case, notwithstanding counsel were not allowed to discuss the constitutionality of the Senate's proceedings, it was very fully discussed by senators themselves. A brief abstract of the debate has been preserved by Mr. Jefferson (Manual, Sec. 3). He says: " In declaring the legality of this order, it was insisted, in support of it, that every man, by the law of nature, and every body of men, possesses the right of self-defense; that *all public functionaries are essentially invested with the powers of self-preservation; that they have an inherent power to do all that is necessary to keep themselves in a condition to discharge the trusts confided to them;* that whatever authorities are given, the means of carrying them into execution are given by necessary implication; *that thus we see the British Parliament exercising the same power; and every court does the same;* that if we have it not, we sit at the mercy of every intruder who may enter our doors or gallery, and, by noise and tumult, render proceeding in business impracticable; that if our tranquility is to be perpetually disturbed by newspapers, etc., it will not be possible to exercise our functions with the requisite coolness and deliberation; and we must therefore have a power to punish those disturbers of our peace and proceedings."

The commitment of John Anderson, in 1818, was followed by an action against the Sergeant-at-Arms of the House of Representatives, for assault and battery and false imprisonment, and at last the power to punish for contempt became the subject of judicial determination. *Anderson* vs. *Dunn*, 6 Wheaton, 204. (1821.)

The defendant pleaded specially, in justification, a resolution and a warrant, which set forth, in general terms only, that the plaintiff had been guilty of a breach of the privileges, and of a contempt of the dignity and authority of the House of Representatives. The legal effect of a mode of pleading which thus omitted to state the nature of the contempt, and whether it was committed in presence of the House or elsewhere, was to set up a power to punish contempts generally; and this claim was conceded by the decision of the Court.

Mr. Justice Johnson, delivering the opinion of the Court, said: "It is certainly true, that there is no power given by the Constitution to either House to punish for contempts, except when committed by their own members. * * Such power, if it exists, must be derived from implication." He then proceeded to state the reasons of the Court for implying it.

Briefly stated, his argument was, that the power to punish this class of injuries belonged to those bodies *ex necessitate,* " on the principle of self-preservation." And he proceeded to say : " In reply to the suggestion that, on this same foundation of necessity, might be raised a superstructure of implied powers in the executive, and every other department and even ministerial officer of the Government, it would be sufficient to observe, that *neither analogy nor precedent* would support the assertion of such powers in any other than a *legislative or judicial body.*"

It was conceded in this opinion that no executive officer could assume and exercise the power of punishment, " on the principle of self-preservation ;" and it was clearly held that a legislative assembly might assume and exercise it on that principle, because it had been determined by precedent to be " necessary" to such bodies as a means of self-preservation.

Mr. Justice Johnson's language did not, it is true, assume the form of an explicit statement of doctrine ; but the inevitable effect of his position was, that each house of our Congress was invested by the Constitution with power to use, for the purpose of self-preservation, whatever means *the common law* had determined to be necessary to that end in the case of legislative assemblies, and that the common law had determined the power to punish obstructors to be necessary to such bodies. If his language should seem to leave any uncertainty on this point, it should be remembered that Mr. Justice Story, who also sat in that case, evidently intended, in his Commentary, to give the same reasons which had prevailed in *Anderson* vs. *Dunn;* and his argument clearly supports this view of the case. He says: " Congress are required to exercise the powers of legislation and deliberation. The safety of the rights of the Nation requires this; and yet, because it is not expressly said that Congress shall possess the appropriate means to accomplish this end, the means are denied and the end may be defeated. * * * * *We may resort to the common law* to aid us in interpreting such instruments and their powers; for that law is the common rule by which all our legislation is interpreted. It furnishes principles equally for civil and criminal justice, for public privileges and private rights. Now, by the common law, power to punish contemps of this nature belongs incidentally to courts of justice and to each house of Parliament. No man ever doubted or denied its existence as to our colonial assemblies in general, whatever may have been thought as to particular exercises of it." Story on the Con., Secs. 845, 846.

It is a very grave matter to question the legality of a practice which has continued from the earliest days of the Constitution to the present time, and the conclusiveness of the great authorities by which that practice has been supported.

If the question had related to the interpretation of particular terms in the Constitution, or to the extent of any express grant of power, early and long continued practice would, without the help of judicial decisions, have been conclusive. And if the grounds on which the power was rested by the decision referred to, had not, since that time, been re-examined by the tribunals of the country from which this doctrine has confessedly been borrowed, and been shown not to have been the basis on which it stood in England, nor to have constituted a general conclusion as to legislative assemblies, and to be therefore incapable to support the assumption of such power by any other legislative assemblies than the houses of Parliament, the question here discussed would have been regarded as closed by judicial authority. But, inasmuch as this claim of power has been based, not upon the interpretation of phrases, but upon general principles which are independent of forms of expression, and of any express grant, it is conceived that long practice is not conclusive. And inasmuch as the question which came before the English tribunal was substantially identical with the question considered in *Anderson* vs. *Dunn*, and has been differently decided, after the most deliberate reconsideration, it is hoped very sincerely that there is no disrespect to our own great tribunal in examining the argument as a question fairly open to discussion. As the result of such an examination it is proposed, in the following remarks, to show:

1st. That on general principle, the power to punish contempts cannot be implied as a power of self-protection, in the case of a legislative assembly.

2d. That the power of the House of Commons to punish for contempts does not stand upon the ground that it is necessary to a legislative assembly, as a power of self-protection; and that its exercise by that body never established a conclusion of the common law that such a power was necessary to legislative assemblies.

3d. That if such a conclusion of the common law had existed, it would have been of no force in determining whether a similar power has, by implication, been granted to each house of our Congress.

4th. That, if such an implication might have been

made on that ground, in the absence of any provision of the Constitution forbidding it, that implication has in fact been forbidden by affirmative provisions of that instrument.

We have first to consider the general principle on which the right of a party to take measures against other persons, for the purpose of self-protection, is based. The following is submitted as an analysis of that principle.

The possessor of a right, whether a private person, a functionary, or a body of functionaries, is entitled to its complete enjoyment, and is therefore entitled to have, in some way, remedies of protection adequate to secure such enjoyment. It is a principle of social organization that, *primarily*, the duty and power to provide remedies of protection belong to the organization itself, as sovereign over all its constituents; and does not belong to any of its constituents except with its consent.

Whether such primary power has been transferred to, and may be exercised by any person or body of persons subject to the sovereignty, is simply a question of fact; and the fact of transfer or permission may be either expressed or implied. An implication that it may be thus exercised may be made on the following grounds: In order to secure *complete* enjoyment of a right, there must be remedies adapted to secure it from interruption or obstruction even for a single moment; that is to say, from being injured at all. A functionary or body of functionaries is entitled, therefore, to remedies which shall instantly put a stop to an obstruction which is occurring, or actually and directly prevent one that is threatened. For example, they are entitled to have persons who are obstructing their functions at once removed, and to have persons who menace such obstructions excluded. But, to require a functionary who is suffering an obstruction, or who is likely to be interrupted, to invoke, for this kind of protection, an external interference, would be to require him to suffer the obstruction meantime, until that interference could be brought into action; and would therefore be to deny him an adequate remedy. Indeed, to just the extent of such enforced endurance, his right *not to be injured at all* would be without any remedy. Since, then, he is entitled to a remedy which shall instantly arrest or perfectly prevent the injury, and since his own hand can furnish that remedy while no other agency can, it follows that the party himself is authorized to provide and apply remedies of this kind. His right to do so is implied from two facts: that he is entitled to an instant cessation of injury; and that the law which established him as a functionary, cannot in any other way furnish him a remedy adequate to that end. In other words, his authority arises *ex necessitate*.

In illustrating this right by example, we have adduced a case in which it accrues because remedies from an external source *arrive too late*. It is conceded, however, that the principle is broad enough to include cases where the only remedies which the law is capable of applying by an external agency, are, in contemplation of law, inadequate for any other reason. The probability of such cases is a matter which it is not necessary to determine. We shall therefore proceed upon an assumption that the right of self-protection stands upon the ground, that the remedy to which the party is entitled cannot be furnished or applied adequately in any other way.

The principle here stated is relied upon because it is found in every civilized system of jurisprudence, and is not peculiar to the common law. In that law itself it is enunciated as a principle of universal recognition. Blackstone, in speaking of the right of self-defense, says: " It [the law] considers that the future process of law is by no means an adequate remedy for injuries accompanied by force; since it is impossible to say to what wanton lengths of rapine or cruelty, outrages of this sort might be carried unless it were permitted a man immediately to oppose one violence with another. Self-defense, therefore, as it is justly called the primary law of nature, so it is not, neither can it be in fact, taken away by the law of society." 3 Bl. 4. And in speaking of the right of a party to abate certain kinds of nuisances, he says : " The reason why the law allows this private and summary method of doing one's self justice, is because injuries of this kind, which obstruct or annoy such things as are of daily convenience or use, require an immediate remedy, and cannot wait the slow progress of the ordinary forms of justice."

And Kent says: "The municipal law of our own country, as well as of every other country, has left with individuals the exercise of the natural right of self-defense, *in all those cases in which the law is either too slow or too feeble to stay the hand of violence.*" 2 Kent, 15.

Since this principle is of universal authority, it must apply to functionaries under our Constitution, and must determine the extent of their power to use measures of self-protection in the discharge of their functions.

It is important, before proceeding to apply it to the matter in question, to recapitulate the elements which unite in constituting the right to do *any particular act* for the purpose of self-protection.

As shown by the recognized operation of the principle, they are as follows:

First, the act to be done for that purpose must operate immediately and directly upon the injury against which protection is sought; being permitted on the very ground that it is necessary as the only means of actually saving the party from being injured at all. Secondly, it must appear that it is his inherent right that *the particular act* which he undertakes to do, should be done by *some* agency. Thirdly, it must appear that this remedy cannot be applied adequately by any other hand than his own; in other words, that there is a necessity, in contemplation of law, that he shall have power to apply it himself.

Assuming these to be the elements of the principle of self-protection, we have next to consider whether power to *punish* comes within that principle.

It is obvious, in the first place, that punishment has no direct action upon injuries, whether past or future. It does not pretend to undo the past injury on account of which it is inflicted; it has regard only to the future, and to possible injuries. But, even as to these, it is only an abuse of words to call it a preventive, in the sense required by the principle of self-protection. Undoubtedly it is characterized in the language of social science as a preventive of wrongs; but it is not regarded even by that science, much less by the law, as having any direct operation toward that end, or any intrinsic capacity to attain it. Its only direct operation is to give warning; to teach a lesson; and that lesson may, or may not, have the secondary effect of diminishing the disposition of wrong-doers to commit injuries. Self-protective remedies are permitted on the ground that they are necessary to the actual saving of the party from being injured; but the capacity, even the tendency of punishment to avert injuries, depends upon the impressionability, the imagination, the audacity, the intelligence, of the persons who are to be warned and instructed by it. It may be inflicted without even touching the result that was hoped for; and the end proves that its office is not actual prevention. Since, then, it operates upon something else than the injury, and is only an educational instrument, calculated to achieve its purpose, not by necessary but only by probable reaction upon the inclination to injure, and thereby upon the injury itself, it cannot be deemed a remedy of self-protection from injury. The latter authorizes a party to deal with a situation, with the wrong which is upon him, or which is approaching; all secondary methods belong to the sovereign, whether a monarch or a community.

In the next place, the principle of self-protection requires that the party should have an inherent right that *the particular act* which he undertakes to do, as a remedy, should be done by *some* agency, either public or private; and it is not an inherent right of an injured party that any particular injury should be *punished*. Whether a particular kind of injury shall be subject to any punishment, and if so in what manner, is essentially a matter of polity, of public discretion; not a matter upon which there can be a foregone conclusion of law. There are very many injuries for which every society deliberately omits to provide any punishment. We have a peculiarly appropriate illustration of this discretion, in the fact to which we shall have occasion to refer in another part of this discussion, that Congress has abolished all punishment for certain injuries which were once punished as contempts of the judicial power of the United States. On the other hand, it is observable that, for those acts which are punished in all communities, the penalties have always varied in degree and method, according to the circumstances and tempers of those communities. In a word, the immemorial and universal practice of mankind has determined that punishment waits upon the judgment and decision of the law-maker, and that it is not to be applied at all, whether by public tribunals or by the hand of the injured party, until the law-maker has prescribed the injuries for which, and the manner in which, it shall be applied. If then, the question whether a particular kind of injury shall be punished at all, is essentially a question of polity, of sovereign discretion, it is impossible that power to inflict punishment should be implied as a power of self-protection, accruing *ex necessitate*.

Finally, power to punish cannot be claimed as a remedy of self-protection on the ground that this remedy will be, in contemplation of law, inadequate, unless it may be applied by the hand of the injured party.

The ground on which self-protective remedies are

most commonly permitted is, that the same remedies applied by any external agency, must arrive too late; that is, after the injury has been accomplished, or unduly protracted. It is sufficient to say that the remedy of punishment necessarily arrives after the injury has been accomplished, whether it is employed by the party or by the common tribunals. As this fact is not altered by permitting the party to exercise the power, no necessity arises that he should be substituted for the common tribunals.

This somewhat elaborate analysis of the general principle of self-protection, which is commonly stated very briefly, has been deemed important, in order to show how many considerations must be overcome by a party who claims that power to punish is, in any particular case, a power of self-protection. A complete reconsideration of a familiar principle sometimes becomes necessary, for the purpose of demonstrating how grave a matter it is to alter its boundaries.

It has been assumed, in making this analysis, that the ordinary principle of self-protection both establishes and limits that right, just as much in the cases of the separate houses of Congress, as in the cases of other functionaries of the Government; unless the self-protective powers of the former are distinguished, by implications of the Constitution, from those of the latter. This was substantially conceded in *Anderson* vs. *Dunn*, and the reasoning of the Court was intended to establish that distinction. We have, therefore, to consider next, whether the Constitution does imply a greater necessity and a larger extent of self-protective power in the cases of our legislative functionaries.

It had been urged by counsel, in *Anderson's* case, that if the principles of self-preservation conferred the power of punishment upon the House of Representatives, they conferred it equally upon the "executive, and every coördinate, and even subordinate, branch of the government." Mr. Justice Johnson, in answer to this proposition, said: "But what is the alternative? The argument leads to the *total annihilation* of the power of the House of Representatives to guard itself from contempts, and leaves it exposed to every indignity and interruption that rudeness, caprice, or even conspiracy, may meditate against it." So in *Duane's* case, it had been said by Senators: "If we have it not [namely, the power to punish], we sit at the mercy of every intruder who may enter our doors or gallery, and, by noise and tumult, render proceeding in business impracticable. If our tranquillity is to be perpetually disturbed by newspaper defamation, it will not be possible to exercise our functions with the requisite coolness and deliberation." And the learned Commentator on the Constitution has declared that "It is obvious that unless such a power, to some extent, exists by implication, it is *utterly impossible* for either House to perform its constitutional functions." Story on the Con., Sec. 845.

If it were true that, unless the power to inflict punishment may be exercised by the House itself, neither House can perform its functions, it would be difficult to resist an implication that such power is conferred by the Constitution; for each House must perform its functions. But it is submitted that the assertions which have been quoted are simply not true. It can be shown, on the contrary, that, without assuming to themselves any such power, those bodies may be perfectly and adequately protected.

In the first place, each House has, upon the principle of self-protection, authority to remove and permanently exclude persons who interrupt its proceedings, or are guilty of indecorum in its presence; and, as it may be provided with such officers as it may need, it may be surrounded with a force which cannot fail to make that power efficient. If it should be found necessary, it may even close its doors and galleries at all times against all persons but its own members and officers. And, as a matter of fact, this admitted right of self-protection has been found to be effective and sufficient for the suppression of every disorder which intruders may create. But power to expel and shut out an intruder is not power to *punish*.

In the next place, it is not true that these bodies must go without that protection which punishment may afford, unless they may inflict such punishment with their own hands. It can be shown that the Constitution authorizes other instrumentalities by which any offense against them may be punished, and that, in contemplation of that instrument—and this must be the conclusive test—punishment so applied is adequate to their protection.

Congress has power to pass "all laws necessary and proper for carrying into execution" any of the powers granted to any department of the government; and, among them, the power of its several houses to perform their respective functions. It is settled that this clause authorizes Congress to provide for the punishment of any wrong whatever which obstructs or impairs the functions of any of these departments; and the Constitution provides the instrumentalities by which such punishment may be awarded and inflicted. It declares that the judicial power of the United States shall be vested in one Supreme Court, and in such inferior courts as Congress may, from time to time, ordain and establish; and that this judicial power shall extend to all cases, in law or equity, arising under the Constitution or laws of the United States. Under these provisions, every act which the several houses of Congress have claimed power *ex necessitate* to punish as a contempt, may be made an offense, and may be punished through the instrumentality of the courts of justice.

That it is at least *lawful* to apply this agency to the protection of those bodies, has not been disputed. It was distinctly admitted by the Court, *arguendo*, in *Anderson* vs. *Dunn*, and it has been affirmed by Congress itself.

The Act of February, 1853 (10 Stat. 171), declared an attempt to bribe a member of either House—the very offense for which, under the name of contempt, Anderson had been punished thirty-five years before—to be a high crime and misdemeanor, subject to indictment and punishable by fine and imprisonment. And the Act of January, 1857 (11 Stat. 155), provided that the refusal of a witness, when summoned before either House, to answer questions pertinent to the matter under inquiry there—an act which both houses assume to punish as a contempt—should be subject to indictment and punishable by imprisonment in a common jail.

It is a settled proposition, then, that these bodies

may, at least, be protected, through the agency of statutes and the courts of justice, against injuries which constitute contempts. The question is solely, therefore, whether this agency must be inadequate. And in determining this question, it is to no purpose to point out practical difficulties in framing a proper statute.

Mr. Justice Johnson assumed that, from their very nature, "the offenses which may be denominated contempts * * * admit of no precise definition," and evidently concluded that a legislative attempt to provide for their punishment would, therefore, be impracticable. It is sufficient answer to say, that, although it may be difficult, it is never impracticable to define by statute every act which it is desirable to punish as an offense. But it is unnecessary to do so; for general words would suffice to describe such offenses. The Judiciary Act, in giving to the Courts of the United States authority to punish this class of injuries, described them simply as "contempts of authority;" and the Crimes' Act of 1790 included a variety of acts under the word "obstructing," when it provided punishment for unlawful interference with service of process. It is not necessary, therefore, to specify every act which may constitute a contempt; nor would such a necessity, if demonstrated, show that legislative definition is impracticable, and therefore inadequate. It may be added, that an implied necessity for a particular jurisdiction over certain matters, on the very ground that the wisdom of the law-maker cannot define them, sounds strangely.

It appears, then, that the ordinary means of affording protection by means of punishment, need not be inadequate because the occasions for punishment are prescribed by express statute. It only remains to inquire whether the ordinary constitutional means of administering punishment so provided, must be inadequate.

It seems to have been assumed that, by a necessity of which the law must take cognizance, legislative bodies are entitled to remedies of protection suitable to their dignity and convenience; and that it is not suitable to either that they should be obliged to call upon the judicial tribunals to punish offenses against them. Of course, this assumption can only be set up as an intendment of the Constitution; since we are dealing with those intendments in determining whether the houses of Congress have this power by implication.

As a matter of fact, this notion that an appeal to other tribunals did not comport with the dignity or convenience of a supreme legislature, is of English origin. Lord Coke and his early successors used to talk of the privileges and powers of Parliament as something which, so far from assuming to protect them, the common law courts might not even presume to know; and even when the ordinary courts of justice came to assert a right to determine what those privileges were, in a case which should enable them to reach the question, they still deemed the protection of them to be a matter not merely out of but above their sphere. Only eleven years before the decision of *Anderson's* case, Lord Ellenborough, in the great case of *Burdett* vs. *Abbott*, 14 East, 1, said: " Could it be expected that they should stand high in the estimation and reverence of the people, if, whenever they were insulted, they were obliged to wait the comparatively slow proceedings of the ordinary course of law for their redress? That the Speaker with his mace should be under the necessity of going before the grand jury to prefer a bill of indictment for the insult offered to the House?" This sentiment very naturally seized upon the imagination of other judges; but with the great lawyers of Lord Ellenborough's own time, the prevailing argument against an appeal tothe or dinary tribunals for protection of privilege was, not that such an appeal was inconsistent with the dignity and convenience of so high a body as Parliament, but that Parliament was itself a High Court, superior to all other courts of the realm, and that there was a legal inconsistency in a resort by a higher to a lower court for protection.

Lord Ellenborough's melo-dramatic picture of what would have been a very simple proceeding—and the judicial method might have been rendered more simple and more expeditious in any degree that Parliament might deem convenient—was alarming enough to every one who inclined to believe that all English institutions were necessary; and very likely it was true that the House of Commons, by laying off its power to punish offenders against its dignity, and thus losing a part of its terrors, would have suffered a temporary loss of prestige. But it is difficult to perceive how such considerations could demonstrate that kind of necessity of which a court must take judicial cognizance, and from which it must make a legal implication of power. They belong to the domain of polity, not to that of jurisprudence. Notwithstanding the peculiar position of Parliament in the British Constitution, they were, as a matter of law, insufficient ground for the assumption of such power by the House of Commons.

But whatever notion Englishmen may have had, as to the powers which dignity made essential to their legislative assemblies, that notion is not to be imported and made a source of power here, unless it is countenanced by our Constitution. For it cannot be too often repeated, we are dealing only with the intendments and implications of that instrument.

The first reflection which suggests itself, on turning to its provisions, is, that a construction which finds there an implication that methods of protection which are consistent with the dignity and convenience of the Executive, are not consistent with those of the Legislature, is not to be stated dogmatically, nor accepted without the most careful consideration. It is conceived that, on the contrary, all of the implications of the Constitution are that the Legislature is not placed, by any exigencies of dignity or convenience, above the application of the common means of protection.

All departments of this Government are the creatures of the Constitution, dependent upon it for existence or power, co-ordinate and independent in operation, equally indispensable to the action of the Government. It is an implication of that supreme law that all of them shall be protected in the exercise of their functions, and that protection of one indispensable department is as essential as protection of another. Methods of protection, by means of punishment, which are lawfully applicable to all of them, have been expressly authorized by it, and to some of them no others can be applied. Is it not an intendment of a law which provides expressly one method, and only one method, by which remedies of protection may be applied, that it has not only provided it for common use, but as a method which is *suitable and adequate* to common use? Before any department of the Government can deny this implication, and can say that the common means of protection, although intended to be used in its behalf, were not regarded by the Constitution as sufficient in its case, it must point out affirmative proof that it is distinguished and placed above the others in dignity by that instrument. Such a relation to the other co-ordinate agencies of the common sovereign is not to be assumed; it must be found in the law which established all of them. And whether it is to be found there, does not depend upon the impression which the departments may make upon the imagination, nor even upon the comparative importance and gravity of their functions. As bodies which participate in the making of laws by which the other agencies of government are bound, these assemblies may seem to exercise a superior function, and thus to be themselves superior. But a law is naught unless it is enforced; and when they carefully distributed these functions, the authors who prescribed them said: " We alone are sovereign; you are only our equal agencies, equally important, equally entitled to protection, and by equal means."

The subordinate ground on which a necessity for this power has sometimes been implied—namely, that, in order to meet the convenience of legislative assemblies, punishment must be summary, and therefore must be applied by themselves, is hardly worthy of discussion. How did it become a necessity that the punishment of this particular class of wrongs should be swifter than all other punishments? When the Constitution is content that even the most perilous wrongs, aimed directly at the life and safety of the whole Nation, such as treason or the counterfeiting of the public securities, shall be triable only upon indictment and by a jury, it would be a strange implication that the same instrument held it to be necessary that a mere insult, or a temporary obstruction offered to a part of the legislature, should be punished without trial and without deliberation, in order to be punished effectively. The fact is, that the argument simply confounds consequence with cause. When a legislative body undertakes to administer punishment, its proceedings are inevitably summary. It is itself the accuser, the prosecutor, and the judge. It has no forms of trial, and, as none but its own members take part in its deliberations, it affords no standing, except by grace, for counsel or defence. The jurisdiction to punish, therefore, was not assumed in order that punishment might be summary, but punishment was summary because the jurisdiction was exercised by a body which must proceed in that way.

It is not pretended that there is any novelty in these arguments against an extraordinary power. They would have been urged with less confidence if they were. They were pressed upon the attention of Congress long ago in *Duane's* case, with an ability and force which cannot be surpassed; and we cannot do better than to present the recapitulation of them which has been left us by Mr. Jefferson. It was urged in the Senate, "that Congress have no such natural or necessary powers, but such as are given to them by the Constitution; that it has given them, directly, exemption from personal arrest, exemption from question elsewhere for what is said in their house, and power over their own members and proceedings; for these no further law is necessary, the Constitution being the law; that, moreover, by that article of the Constitution which authorizes them 'to make all laws necessary and proper for carrying into execution' the powers vested by the Constitution in them, they may provide by law for an undisturbed exercise of their functions; for example, for the punishment of contempts, of affrays or tumults in their presence, &c.; but, till the law be made, it does not exist, and does not exist from their own neglect; that, in the meantime, however, they are not unprotected, the ordinary magistrates and courts of law being open and competent to punish all unjustifiable disturbances and defamations; and even their own sergeant, who may appoint deputies *ad libitum* to aid him, is equal to small disturbances; that in requiring a previous law, the Constitution had regard to the inviolability of the citizen as well as of the member; as, should one house, in the regular form of a bill, aim at too broad privileges, it may be checked by the other, and both by the President; and also as, the law being promulgated, the citizen will know how to avoid offence. But if one branch may assume its own privileges without control, if it may do it on the spur of the occasion, conceal the law in its own breast, and, after the fact committed, make its sentence both the law and the judgment on that fact; if the offence is to be kept undefined, and to be declared only *ex re nata*, and according to the passions of the moment, and there be no limitation either in the manner or measure of the punishment, the condition of the citizen would be perilous indeed." Jeff. Man., Sec. 3.

It has been observed that this re-examination of a question which has been judicially determined, would not have been undertaken, had not the grounds on which that decision was partly based been since disapproved by other tribunals of high authority. That observation referred to English decisions, which will be cited in their proper place. But it may be remarked at this point, that the conclusiveness of *Anderson's* case has been impliedly questioned by a very high authority in our own country.

In 1860 the case of *Sanborn* vs. *Carlton*, 15 Gray, 399, occasioned a very full discussion, before the Supreme Court of Massachusetts, of the power of the Senate of the United States to commit for contempt. The case was disposed of on other grounds, without a decision of that question; but the remarks which Chief Justice Shaw may be said to have seized opportunity to make, indicate plainly that, in the opinion of that very great judge, the whole matter was open to further discussion, and that he by no means regarded the authority of *Anderson* vs. *Dunn* as conclusive. He said:

"This question is a very broad and important one, and opens many interesting questions as to the functions and power of the United States Senate, as a constituent part of the executive and legislative departments of the United States Government, and the modes in which they are to be exercised, and the limits by which they are qualified.

"It is admitted in the arguments that there is no express provision in the Constitution of the United States, giving authority in terms; but it is maintained that it is necessarily incident to various authorities vested in the Senate of the United States, in its legislative, executive, and judicial functions, and must therefore be held to be conferred by necessary implication.

"These questions manifestly requiring great deliberation and research, in order to come to a satisfactory conclusion, and some preliminary questions having been suggested by the petitioner's counsel, it was proposed, and not objected to by the learned District Attorney and Assistant District Attorney of the United States, by whom the court were attended in behalf of the respondents, to consider these preliminary questions first; because, if the objections, on the face of them, were sustained, it would supersede the necessity of discussing the other questions arising in the case."

The learned and careful judge who made these observations, would hardly have spoken of the question of incidental power, as one "requiring great deliberation and research, in order to come to a satisfactory conclusion," and have intimated, as he did, an intention to discuss that question, in case he should not sustain the preliminary objections, had not the reasoning and judgment in *Anderson* vs. *Dunn* failed, in his opinion, to furnish a satisfactory conclusion.

Before we proceed to the next branch of this

inquiry, it should be repeated that, in order to base this power upon an implication from necessity, it must appear that such necessity exists in the judgment of the Constitution. It would so exist if the general principle of self-protection included power to inflict punishment; or if, by any express provision of that instrument, or by its omission to afford other means of protection, an implication might be made that it conceded, in the case of the two houses of Congress, a necessity for larger and peculiar power, for the purpose of self-protection. But the general principle of self-protection does not include power to punish, and we have not found in the Constitution any indication that it distinguishes between the necessities of those bodies, in the matter of protection, and the necessities of other functionaries. One more ground, on which this intendment of a larger necessity has been based, remains to be considered. It has been claimed, namely, that the Constitution must have intended that the legislative assemblies created by it, should have such power as precedent had established to be necessary to such bodies, and that precedent had established such a necessity in regard to the power in question.

II.

It has been assumed that, at the time of the adoption of the Constitution of the United States, the existence of such a necessity had become a conclusion of law by force of precedents supposed to be had in view by the framers of that instrument. This was substantially the meaning of Mr. Justice Johnson, when he said: "In reply to the suggestion that, on this same foundation of necessity, might be raised a superstructure of implied powers in the executive and every other department, and even in ministerial officers of the Government, it would be sufficient to observe, that neither analogy nor *precedent* would support the assertion of such powers in any other than a legislative or judicial body." Of course, he meant that precedent did support and establish the assertion of the necessity in the latter cases.

This use of precedent has been more explicitly stated by Mr. Bishop, in his work on Criminal Law. He says: "As a matter of natural reason, we know that a court of justice and a legislative body must alike be entrusted with the means to preserve order; else neither the one nor the other could do its business. But by what means? This is a question on which men will differ; therefore the law steps in and points to 'immemorial usage,' and says, that *the power which has been immemorially exercised shall be taken as the measure of necessity in the case.* In other words and to apply the proposition to the case in hand, the law says that the power which the House of Commons has exercised, in cases of contempts of its authority and of the privileges of its members—conceded to be just on all hands—from the beginning of things, is *the law's measure* of what is necessary and proper to be possessed by a legislative body similarly situated." Bishop, Crim. Law, Vol. 2, Sec. 249, note 4 (Ed. 1872).

This passage referred to the implied powers of colonial assemblies, and of the State Legislatures; but the same reasoning, as we have seen, has been applied to the houses of Congress. The argument in the latter case has claimed substantially that, when the Constitution gave to these bodies, by implication, whatever powers were necessary to the exercise of their functions, it had been determined in an authoritative manner that power to punish contempts offered them was necessary to that end. Practically, the meaning of this proposition was, that the common law had determined that the power which it gave to the House of Commons was necessary to a legislative assembly.

It is plain that this example, imitated by legislative assemblies in this country before the adoption of the Constitution, is the real ground on which this claim of power for the two houses of Congress is supported: its advocates have never ventured to base it wholly upon the ordinary principle of self-preservation. It is of the utmost importance, therefore, to ascertain the ground on which the power of the House of Commons itself stood; and for this purpose it will be necessary to consider the history of that body. After a candid attempt to make such an examination, we venture, at the outset, to assert that the exercise of this power by that assembly does not even tend to show that it is incident *ex necessitate* to all legislative assemblies; and that it accrued to the House of Commons simply because the British Constitution did not furnish those assured and effective means of external protection which the Constitution of the United States does furnish.

It has invariably been assumed that the power of the House of Commons to adjudicate and inflict punishment for contempts and breaches of privilege was of immemorial usage. This was chiefly important in order to establish its *legality;* and for that purpose Lord Ellenborough stated very elaborately, in the famous case of *Burdett* vs. *Abbott*, 14 East. 1, the method of setting out the prescription. But immemorial usage has been strongly urged for another purpose—namely, as establishing a conclusion of the common law, that such power was inherent in the very constitution of a legislative assembly, and existed, *ex necessitate*. It is important first, therefore, to inquire into the antiquity of this power of the House of Commons.

Before we take up the specific proofs touching this question, it may be observed that the general history of the Commons would hardly lead us to suppose that they would come very early to exercise an independent means of vindicating their privileges or dignity. All the circumstances of their early place in the Constitution make it improbable that they should do so. For a considerable period their chief business as a legislative body was to vote subsidies; and even when the authority of their name was used in making laws, they were only petitioners.

The learned Mr. Spence's sketch of the methods of parliamentary action presents a picture in which the whole Parliament, Lords as well as Commons, seem to stand in shadow; a picture in which they stand asking for rights, not vindicating them. We venture to quote from his account at some length: "Prior to the reign of Edward I (1272), laws appear to have been drawn up and proposed to Parliament by the King. After the representatives of the Commons were admitted as members of the Parliament, a mode was opened to the community at large for having their petitions presented and attended to. The laws, from this time, usually originated in petitions presented by the Commons, or by the Lords and Commons, to the King, or to the King and his council. The statutes were drawn up after the end of each Parliament, from such of the petitions and the answers as were considered fit to be converted into permanent laws; and after having been shown to the King, and his consent obtained, they were entered on the Rolls of Parliament. Writs, in the name of the King, were then sent into every county, with directions to have the statute proclaimed. So that the statutes, whether they originated with the King or not, very commonly assumed the form of royal ordinances, or concessions from the King, and were promulgated as proceeding from the royal authority alone.

"In the reign of Edward III (1327–1377) the following form was usually adopted: 'These be the articles *accorded* in the Parliament of our Lord the King, by our said Lord the King, with the assent of the Prelates, Earls, and Barons, and also at the request of the Knights of the Shires and of the Commons, by their petitions put in the said Parliament;' though this form is not uniformly adhered to. * * *

"Many inconveniences arose to the subject, and numerous irregularities were occasioned, from the ancient mode of framing and publishing the statutes; sometimes no statute was made, though agreed on; things agreed on were occasionally omitted; sometimes things neither prayed for nor agreed on were added; and sometimes entire statutes were made, to which neither Lords nor Commons had assented. The Commons, in the reign of Henry IV (1399–1413), petitioned for a remedy for these inconveniences and abuses; and the King, in answer, conceded that in future the clerks of the Parliament should draw up the Acts, with the advice of the Justices, from the substance of the proceedings, and then show them to the King for his assent.

"In the succeeding reign (Henry V, 1413–1422) the King, in answer to a petition of the Commons, conceded that nothing should be enacted on the petition of the Commons that was contrary to their asking, whereby they should be bound without their consent. But the due enactment of laws, as assented by the Lords and Commons, was for the first time effectually secured by the practice which obtained in the reign of Edward IV (1461–1483), and has continued ever since, of reducing the petition or bill into the form of an Act, and presenting it in that state for the royal assent, or rather, as it should be called, *fiat*, looking to the terms in which that assent is conveyed.

"From the reign of Henry VII downwards, the statutes have been uniformly drawn up as made with the assent and by the authority of the Commons equally as of the Lords; though the imperial style is still so far preserved, that the sovereign enacts by the special authority of the Lords and Commons in the particular case." 1 Spence Eq. Jur., 263-272.

Such a picture as this does not prepare us to credit the assumption that the present privileges or powers of the House of Commons were conceded by a formal statute in the time of Henry III. . A body which, at the beginning, attended Parliament only to say whether it would be taxed, and afterwards played only the part of petitioners in matters of general legislation; attaining the position of equal *authority* with the Lords after two hundred years of existence, was not likely to take very high ground concerning its privileges until it found itself set well upon its feet. The claim that its present privileges, and, *a fortiori*, the claim that its peculiar jurisdiction for the protection of those privileges, was actually of immemorial usage, coincident with its action as a legislative assembly, would be rejected by a disinterested reader of English history as wholly inconsistent with known facts, and even if no specific disproof existed. But specific disproof does exist. The recorded precedents, which have been collected by Hatsell, show that centuries elapsed after the establishment of the House of Commons, before that body took into its hands the vindication and protection of even its most indispensable privileges. And we shall find that, during all that time, the Commons were dependent, for protection, upon the King, or upon the King and the Lords, or upon the common law courts; and that they were protected only by civil remedies.

In 9 Edw. II (1316) the Prior of Melton, whose

parliamentary privilege had been violated, resorted to a remedy which placed the matter on the footing of a private injury. 1 Hatsell, 12. This proceeding was by an original writ of attachment, returnable into the King's Bench; and, as Mr. Holroyd said in the argument of *Burdett* vs. *Abbott*, it appears plainly to have been an action for a trespass and a breach of privilege also; the matter complained of being the distraining of the plaintiff, by his horses and harness, at York, while returning from the Parliament at Lincoln. The manner in which the privilege was alleged is important; it was set out in the form of a recital of *the King's obligation* to protect the prelates, earls, barons et alios, tam clericos quam laicos, against all grievances. The process was executed and the defendants were attached, but no judgment upon it has been found; so that the result of the case does not appear. The fact, however, that an *action* was brought for that which was complained of as a breach of privilege of Parliament, as well as a trespass, and that the defendants, who might have had a good cause for distraining, except so far as respected the breach of privilege, were put to answer both, informs us of the condition of the law at that time touching the matter of protection.

The next case was in 5 Hen. IV (1404), 1 Hatsell, 13, where the Commons addressed a petition to the King, praying his protection of their privilege, in language which frankly describes a dependence which was actual, not theoretical. They set forth that, according to the custom of the realm, they and their servants attended Parliament *under the King's special protection and defense*, and that divers of their members, and the servants of members, had been arrested in coming to and during Parliament, "*en contempt de vous*, grande *damage de partie*, et retardacion des besoignes de vos Parliamentz," and thereupon prayed that persons causing such arrests should pay a fine to the King and treble damages to the party aggrieved. The answer, through the Lords, refused the prayer, because a sufficient remedy already existed. What this sufficient remedy was, is not clear; but it has been suggested (1 Hatsell, 14) that it was merely the writ of privilege or habeas corpus. The writ of privilege issued out of chancery, and was merely for the release of the member. It was not claimed that such injuries were a *contempt* of Parliament; they were a "retardacion" of its business, while the contempt affected the King. All that the Commons asked was that *he* should punish such offenders, and that the aggrieved member should be compensated; and this was deemed unnecessary. In the same year, on the occasion of *Chedder's* case, the Commons, setting forth that they and their servants were often subjected to personal injuries; for example, murder, mayhem, and battery, and that there was no sufficient remedy, prayed that the King should provide such remedy. In response, it was ordered that persons so offending, were to appear *before the King's Bench* and then be adjudged to pay damages and a fine.

In 8 Hen. VI (1430), 1 Hatsell, 17, one *William Larke*, servant of a member, was committed to the Fleet, in execution of a judgment of the King's Bench recovered before time of Parliament. The Commons, reciting their privilege, pray the King "to order, by the authority of your Parliament, that said *William Larke* be delivered from your said prison" (saving to the plaintiff her execution), and also to grant by the same authority that none of your lieges, the Lords, knights for counties, citizens or burgesses, called to your Parliament, their servants or domestics, be arrested or detained in prison in time of Parliament, unless for treason, felony, or surety of the peace." The King simply granted, by the authority of Parliament, that Larke should be delivered out of prison.

No one seems to have imagined yet any contempt of Parliament, and it would seem to have been thought that the privilege against arrests was too broadly claimed. Hatsell says of this case: "The Commons certainly declare it to be their opinion, that they had clearly the privilege of being free from *all* arrests, during the Parliament, except for treason, felony, or surety of the peace. But when at the close of the petition they pray that for the future it may be enacted into a law that no knights, citizens or burgesses, or their servants, may be arrested or detained in prison during the time of Parliament, except for treason, felony, or surety of the peace, the King refuses their request, and gives a parliamentary negative; and therefore the more natural conclusion to be drawn, as well from the petition as from the King's answer, appears to be that this was not acknowledged to be law, *in the extent* in which the Commons laid it down."

When this precedent was cited in *Arundel's* case, the Lords said of it, that the petition might well be refused, because it asked more than the privilege; *Larke's* imprisonment being *before* time of Parliament; but it should be observed that it was chiefly for a more effective remedy that the Commons asked; and Hatsell well suggests that the King could easily have granted part of the prayer. Plainly there was no haste to magnify the Commons.

Two years later, 1432 (1 Hatsell, 22); they pray the King to order, by authority of Parliament, that if any trespass, offense, or damage shall be done to the persons of knights, citizens, or burgesses, or to their servants, come to Parliament, the party aggrieved may have a writ of trespass against him who shall commit the wrong, returnable into the King's Bench, and thereupon have double damages. It was still only a private action that they proposed; but they thought that the damages should amount to a penalty. But the King refused, leaving the Commons to the law as it stood already. That is to say, they could recover only common damages, as had been allowed in 5 Hen. IV.

The next precedent, which occurred in 11 Hen. VI (1433), is introduced by Hatsell with the following remark: "However, the next year, the same mischief continuing, and it being found necessary, from the frequent assaults made on members attending their duty in Parliament, to apply some more speedy and effectual remedy than what the common law allowed, the House of Commons again are obliged to petition the King for redress." 1 Hatsell, 24.

Reciting first the statute in *Chedder's* case, they then set forth an assault upon Richard Quatermains, one of the knights for Oxford; and thereupon pray that a statute be passed that, in case of an assault upon a member, proclamation shall be made where the offense occurred, requiring the offender to appear before the King's Bench; where, upon default to appear, or appearing and being found guilty, he shall be adjudged to pay double damages. The Commons had greatly moderated their earlier demands, though their grievances had become more frequent and violent. This time their prayer was granted, and from this petition and answer was drawn up, and entered on the Statute Roll, the Act of 11 Hen. VI.

After citing this precedent, Hatsell remarks: "Notwithstanding these repeated acts of Parliament to secure the members of both houses from any insults on their persons, such was the licentiousness of the times—or, rather, so slow and ineffectual were the remedies given by these laws—that in a very few years the Commons again apply to the King for further provisions to suppress this very dangerous practice." 1 Hatsell, 27. This time they pray for the same writ of proclamation that had been allowed at that Parliament to Sir Thomas Parr; but what that writ was is not known.

We come next to *Thorpe's* case, 31 and 32 Hen. VI (1454), in which there was a total denial of remedy, and even the privilege itself of the Commons House was treated with contempt by the Lords. A judgment had been recovered by the Duke of York against the Speaker of the House of Commons, in an action of trespass brought into the Court of Exchequer, and the Speaker was taken in execution and committed to the Fleet, as well for the fine due to the King, as for the damages adjudged to the plaintiff. Upon the meeting of Parliament, the Commons petitioned *the King and the Lords* that they might enjoy all such liberties and privileges as they had been accustomed and of ancient times used, for coming to Parliament, and going and returning; and then they required that their Speaker might have his liberty; this being declared to be a privilege *of Parliament.* The Lords, assuming entire control of the matter, consulted the Judges, who, with a protestation that it was not for them to determine the privileges "of the High Court of Parliament," proceeded to state what they would do if the matter came before their courts upon a writ of privilege, and in this indirect manner they informed the Lords that the Speaker had privilege to be released from arrest. Nevertheless, the record shows that it was "concluded by the Lords" that Thorpe should remain in prison according to law—which meant according to the common law—notwithstanding the privilege of Parliament and the fact that he was Speaker. The answer of the Lords "being a matter of law," was communicated to the Commons by one of the law officers attending the House, and thereupon the Commons were actually enjoined to proceed without delay to choose a new Speaker. And this was done. Little delay, indeed, marred any part of this extraordinary proceeding; for only three days elapsed between the petition of the Commons and their election of a Speaker. The violation of privilege was flagrant and contemptuous, and the decision of the Lords has ever since been conceded to have been monstrous; yet even in such a case it was not imagined by the Commons that they possessed any means of helping themselves.

When this case was referred to in the debate on the 8th of March, 1620, Sir N. Rich said: "It is a case begotten by the iniquity of the times, when the Duke of York might have had an overgrown power in it," and doubtless the Duke had much to do with the conclusion of the Lords; for he was present in their House during the whole proceeding. But the "iniquity of the times" does not account for the fact that the Commons proceeded by petition. *That* proceeding had been their uniform course when one of their members was arrested.

Hatsell points out that their course, in petitioning as well the Lords as the King, was an extraordinary feature in this case; but there would seem to have been good reason for such a departure from custom. Henry must have been, at that time, disabled by one of his fits of insanity. The Duke had opened that Parliament on the 14th of February, 1454, "as lieutenant or commissioner for the King," and may already have been elected by it "to be protector and defender of the realm of England."

In the next case which occurred, 39 Hen. VI (1461), the petition of the Commons was addressed to the King alone. It asked for a special statute to enable the Lord Chancellor to release *Walter Clerke*, one of their members, from imprisonment on execution. 1 Hatsell, 41.

Fourteen years later, 14 Edw. IV (1475), a similar petition was made in the case of *Edward Hyde*, a member. This precedent is noticeable because, only two years before that time, the Court of Exchequer had held, in the case of *John Walsh*, "that a member was not liable to be imprisoned for debt, sitting the Parliament." Such a judgment would seem to mean that the imprisonment, even in execution, was *illegal*. If that were so, a special act would not be necessary for the purpose of saving the Sheriff from liability for releasing the prisoner, or of saving the plaintiff's execution. Yet the Commons, who must have known of that decision, only asked for Hyde's release, and on the usual terms. Hatsell therefore expresses the opinion that imprisonment of a member on execution could not, at that time, have been *illegal*, and that there was no other redress than a special act of Parliament. 1 Hatsell, 47, 48. Up to this time, then, it would seem that, so far from the House of Commons having independent remedies of its own, even its very privilege was trammelled by the process of the common-law courts, and that when the latter was used in execution, it could not be set aside or superseded, except by an act of the whole Parliament.

These precedents, running through a period of one hundred and sixty years, from 1315 to 1475, show— 1st. That the only privilege claimed by the Commons was freedom and safety for themselves, and their servants attending them, in coming to, continuing at, and returning from Parliament; including under this head, in one or two instances, an exemption of their necessary goods. 2d. That, for protection in this privilege, they were, both in fact and according to their own theory, dependent upon the King and his courts of common law, or upon the King and the Lords in Parliament. 3d. That the only remedies provided for a violation of this privilege were, a mere release from imprisonment, or an award of damages; in some cases penal. These conclusions are fully sustained by the English writers on Parliamentary law. Mr. Hatsell, in speaking of the period which came down to 39 Hen. VI, says: "The privileges claimed by the House of Commons during this period, were only for the knights, citizens, and burgesses, and their menial servants or *familiares*, present with them in their attendance on Parliament. 2. The duration of these privileges is in no instance carried further than in their coming, staying, and returning to their homes. 3. The extent of the privilege claimed is, to be free from any assaults, or from arrests and imprisonments, except for treason, etc." 1 Hatsell, 38. And, in speaking of the remedies for violation of these privileges, as they stood even three-quarters of a century later, he says: "Hitherto we have seen that when a member, or his servant, has been imprisoned, the House of Commons have never proceeded to deliver such person out of custody by virtue of their own authority; but, if the member has been in execution, have applied for an act of Parliament to enable the Chancellor to issue his writ for his release, or, if the party was confined only on mesne process, he has been delivered by his writ of privilege, which he was entitled to at common law." 1 Hatsell, 53. And Sir Thomas Erskine May, who would not hastily impugn the antiquity of any Parliamentary privilege or power, frankly describes the earlier condition of the law in similar terms. He says: "In treating of the privileges of individual members, it will be shown that, in the earlier periods of Parliamentary history, the Commons did not always vindicate their privileges by their own direct authority; but resorted to the King, to special statutes, to writs of privilege, and even to the House of Lords, to assist them in protecting themselves. It will be seen in what manner they *gradually assumed* their just position, as an independent part of the Legislature, and at length established the present mode of administering the law of Parliament." May's Parl. Law, 69. (a)

The first of the steps by which the Commons "gradually assumed" the powers and privileges, which are now claimed to be of "immemorial usage," was taken in the case of *George Ferrers*, which occurred 34 Hen. VIII (1543).

As the date of this step is of some importance, it is proper, before stating that case, to correct a citation which Lord Ellenborough is reported to have made in *Burdett* vs. *Abbott*. Evidently intending to cite the cases in chronological order, he says: "I would refer only generally to the case of *Ferrers* (very fully reported in Crompton's Jurisdiction of Courts); *Trewinnard's* case, in Dy. 59; William *Thranwis's* case, in 1529, who was committed to the custody of the Sergeant-at-Arms, for a contempt in words against the dignity of the House; etc." No such case as Thranwis's is mentioned either by Hatsell or May,

---

(a) Mr. Holroyd, whose statements, even in the argument of a cause, may be regarded as authority, pointed out, in the argument of *Burdett* vs. *Abbott*, that in the time of Henry VII the House of Commons, so far from inflicting punishment for breach of their privileges, did not even act upon their own authority in delivering a member imprisoned contrary to privilege. In citing the case of *Roo* vs. *Sadcliffe*, 1 Hen. VII, he said: "Up to that period the House of Commons had never proceeded as for a breach of privilege upon their own authority. When it was a common case of privilege known to the law, a writ of privilege was issued as a matter of course, by which it was enforced: when there was any doubt or difficulty in the matter it was referred to the consideration of the whole Parliament, and acted upon by them as a matter of common concern to both houses; but it never was acted upon by the Commons alone on their single resolution: they had never proceeded to deliver any person arrested upon process out of custody by their own authority: on the contrary, they had at last abandoned their repeated claim and privilege to be exempt from being *impleaded* during Parliament, after it had been as often disallowed by the Lords and the judges." 14 East. 1.

and the name and date of the case are undoubtedly wrong. The learned Judge intended, of course, to refer to the case of *William Thrower*, which occurred, not in 1529, but in 1559. Thrower, who was a servant of the Master of the Rolls, was called before the bar of the House for having said at Lincoln's Inn, that if a certain ridiculous bill about women's head gear were introduced in the Commons they would make a question of it; and that he had heard some of the Lords say so at his master's table. It was in the latter statement that the sting lay, and poor Thrower had to suffer vicariously. But it was not upon any such matter as that, that the power to punish for contempt would be used, until it had grown somewhat familiar by use. As the real occasion of its first exercise, as well as the date, are of some moment, it has been deemed worth while to correct what is probably only a printer's error.

We return then, to *Ferrers'* case, as the original of this power. The following account of it is taken by Hatsell from Holinshed's Chronicles:

"In the Lent season, whilst the Parliament yet continued, one *George Ferrers*, Gentleman, servant to the King, being elected a burgess for the town of Plimmouth, in the county of Devon, in going to the Parliament House, was arrested in London by a process out of the King's Bench, at the suit of one White, for the sum of two hundred marks, or thereabouts, wherein he was late afore condemned as surety for the debt of one Weldon of Salisbury; which arrest being signified to Sir Thomas Moile, Knight, then Speaker of the Parliament, and to the Knights and Burgesses there, order was taken that the Sergeant of the Parliament, called S. J., should forthwith repair to the Counter, in Bread Street, whither the said Ferrers was carried, and there to demand delivery of the prisoner. Thereupon the Sergeant, as he had in charge, went to the Counter and declared to the Clerks there what he had in commandment; but they, and other officers of the city, were so far from obeying the said commandment, as, after many stout words, they forcibly resisted the said Sergeant; whereof ensued a fray within the Counter gates, between the said Ferrers and the said officers, not without hurt of either part; so the said Sergeant was driven to defend himself with his mace of armes, and had the crown thereof broken by bearing off a stroke, and his man stroken down. During this brawle, the Sheriffs of London, called Rowland Hill and H. Suckley, came hither; to whom the Sergeant complained of this injury; and required of them the delivery of the said Burgess, as afore; but they bearing with their officers, made little account either of his complaint or of his message, rejecting the same contemptuously, with much proud language, so as the Sergeant was forced to return without the prisoner; and finding the Speaker and all the Knights and Burgesses set in their places, declared unto them the whole cause as it fell out: who took the same in so ill part, that they altogether (of whom there were not a few, as well of the King's Privy Council, as also of his Privy Chamber) would sit no longer without their Burgess, but rose up wholly and retired to the Upper House; where the whole case was declared by the mouth of the Speaker, before Sir Thomas Audley, Knight, then Lord Chancellor of England, and all the Lords and

Judges there assembled; *who, judging the contempt
to be very great, referred the punishment thereof to the
order of the Commons House.*

"They, returning to their places again, upon new
debate of the case, took order that their Sergeant
should eftsoon repaire to the Sheriffs of London and
require delivery of the said Burgess, without any writ
or warrant had for the same, but only as aforesaid:
Albeit the Lord Chancellor offered there to grant a
writ, which they of the Commons House refused;
being of a clear opinion that all commandments and
other acts proceeding from the Neather House were
to be done and executed by the Sergeant without
writ, only by show of his mace, which was his warrant. But before the Sergeant's return into London,
the Sheriffs having intelligence how haynously the
matter was taken, became somewhat more milde, so
as, upon the said second demand, they delivered the
prisoner without any denial. But the Sergeant having
then further in commandment from those of the
Neather House, charged the said Sheriffs to appear
personally on the morrow, by eight of the clock,
before the Speaker of the Neather House, and bring
thither the Clerks of the Counter, and such other of
their officers as were parties to the said affray, and in
like manner to take into custody the said White,
which wittingly procured the said arrest, in contempt
of the privilege of the Parliament. Which commandment being done by the said Sergeant accordingly,
on the morrow the two Sheriffs, with one of the
Clerks of the Counter (which was the chief occasion
of the said affray), together with the said White,
appeared in the Commons House: when the Speaker

charging them with their contempt and misdemeanor aforesaid, they were compelled to make immediate answer, with out being admitted to any counsell; albeit Sir R. Cholmley, then Recorder of London, and other counsell of the city there present offered to speak in the cause, which were all put to silence, and none suffered to speak but the parties themselves; whereupon in the conclusion the said Sheriffs, and the same White, were committed unto the Tower of London, and the said Clerk (which was the occasion of the fray) to a place there called Little Ease, and the officer of London, which did the arrest, called Bayley, with four officers more, to Newgate, where they continued from 28th until 30th of March: and then they were delivered, not without humble suit made by the Lord Mayor of London and other friends.

"The King, being then advertised of all this proceeding, called immediately before him the Lord Chancellor of England and his judges, with the Speaker of the Parliament and other the gravest persons of the Neather House, to whom he delivered his opinion to this effect: First commending their wisdom in maintaining the privileges of their house (which he would not have to be infringed in any point), alleged that he, being head of the Parliament, and attending in his own person upon the business thereof, ought in reason to have privilege for him and all his servants attending there upon him. So that if the said Ferrers had been no Burgess, but only his servant, that in respect thereof he was to have the privilege as well as any other: * * and we are informed by our Judges, that we at no time stand so highly in our estate royale, as in the time of Parliament, wherein we as head, and you as members, are conjoined and knit together in one body politic, so as whatsoever offence or injury (during that time) is offered to the meanest member of the House, *is to be judged as done against our person and the whole Court of Parliament;* which prerogative of the Court is so great (as our learned counsell informeth us), as all acts and processes coming out of any other inferior courts must for the time cease and give place to the highest."

The authenticity of this case has been questioned; probably because the first report of it is found in Holinshed's Chronicles. Hatsell mentions in a note (Vol. I, p. 57) that: " In Carte's History of England, Vol. III, pp. 164, 541, it is said: 'That the whole case of Ferrers, related by Holinshed and copied by Grafton and Speed, is untrue.' Carte supposes the case to be a mere fable, which the Puritans and Calvinists prevailed upon Holinshed to insert in his history to serve some political purpose." Like enough both parties colored highly in those days; but, as Holinshed's book appeared in 1577, only thirty-four years after the alleged date of *Ferrers'* case, it is not probable that even the most unscrupulous partisan would venture so soon to create a parliamentary event. It would be well remembered whether the Lords and Commons took the courses ascribed to them. Besides, we find Holinshed's report reproduced in Crompton's Jurisdiction of Courts, which was printed in 1592; and Crompton vouches for his own precautions and accuracy in these words: " Because this case hath been diversely reported, and is *commonly alleged as a precedent* for the privilege of Parliament, I have endeavoured myself to learn the truth thereof, and to set it forth with the whole circumstances at large, according to their instructions who ought best to know and remember it." The lapse of forty-nine years could not have removed all witnesses capable of remembering so marked a change in Parliamentary action; and many lawyers must have been living in Crompton's time who might have learned the facts from those who actually witnessed them. The very diversity of reports with which he had met, was more likely to happen in the tradition of an actual event than in fiction; and his statement that he had the facts from persons who remembered them must be accepted as conclusive proof, unless it is overcome by positive disproof, or by an extreme improbability that such a case could occur. Neither of these appears. Carte's disbelief is not disproof; and as to probability, we know that a change had taken place, and that power to punish as a contempt, such acts at least as were committed in *Ferrer's* case, had been assumed by the House of Commons. As to the time when this change occurred, we know that it must have been before the year 1552, when the power was unquestionably exercised in *Creketoste's* case. 1 Hatsell, 71. There is no reason, therefore, to doubt the authenticity of Holinshed's account of *Ferrers'* case.

We have now followed the precedents through a period of two hundred and thirty-six years, from 1316 to 1552, and may gather from them several important conclusions.

1st. A breach of the privileges of the House of

Commons was undoubtedly understood to constitute a contempt of the privileges of Parliament, and no doubt was punishable; but no instance has been found of such contempt having been punished by any authority whatever prior to 1543. For almost three centuries, the protection of the Commons seems to have been confined to a mere release of their members from imprisonment and to a recovery of damages.

2d. It appears that, prior to the year 1543, it was understood that, although a contempt of the privileges enjoyed by the Commons might be punished, the law of the realm did not vest in them an independent authority and jurisdiction to inflict such punishment. The action of the Commons in appealing to the Lords in *Ferrers'* case, the action of the Lords in "referring the punishment" to the Commons, and the action of the King in communicating his approval of what had been done, are conclusive evidence on this point.

3d. It appears that, when the Commons undertook to exercise that jurisdiction, they acquired it substantially by grant, and that the matter was so understood by themselves and by the Lords and by the King. On this point, also, their appeal to the Lords, the reference of the matter to them by the Lords, and the King's peculiar manner of sanctioning the whole proceeding, are conclusive evidence. It is not important to determine how nearly the actual, though informal, consent of all the branches of Parliament was equivalent to a statute of the realm, for the purpose of conferring the power; it is enough that it accrued to the Commons practically by concession, and as something which they were well understood not to possess already. When the question is, whether the power was inherent in the House of Commons, as a power necessarily incident to the constitution of a legislative assembly for the purposes of self-protection, or was the mere creature of law—in other words, whether it was *ex necessitate* or was merely *lawful*—it is immaterial that the formalities of legislation were not observed. Other constitutional powers of that house have grown up in an equally informal manner, but are nevertheless held to have been established by law.

4th. It appears that, in accordance with the patchwork method of the British Constitution, this grant was in effect a Constitutional distribution of power, and that it came to pass because the Constitution had hitherto failed to provide any sufficient means for the protection of the Commons. It was impossible, by reason of the interests of other powers in the State, to furnish such protection in any other way. It could not be administered by the Courts; for the Constitution could not at that time provide an independent judiciary. It could not be administered by means of special acts, for legislation was a matter of discretion, and might not be obtained. In short, this was the only provision which the British Constitution of that time could make. The result does not even tend to demonstrate that such a power and jurisdiction was inherent in, and belonged *ex necessitate*, to a legislative body.

Of course, it is not pretended, in characterizing that proceeding as a constitutional distribution of power, that it was deliberately and consciously undertaken for that purpose. It is only in looking back upon the history of the Commons, that the actual forces and reasons which brought about this, like other changes, can be appreciated. Considered from that point of view, it was as much a part of English constitution-making, as other powers of the House of Commons.

It is not for a moment denied that there was a *necessity* that the House of Commons should acquire this power, and that they should possess it as a means of self-protection. But it is insisted that that necessity was peculiar to its position among the contending powers of the State, and that it would not have arisen if the antagonistic powers had been willing to provide other means.

That such a step, apparently towards independence, should have been achieved in the last years of Henry VIII, may seem to be a matter of some wonder; for the student of English History would hardly look to that period for any development of parliamentary powers which should render either the Lords or the Commons less dependent upon the King. Both bodies usurped enormously to further his will; but against it they dared not claim their own. Their relation to him, in legislative matters, was simply that of shameful servility, and it is difficult to decide which of them was readier to degrade itself. But the explanation is not wanting; and the accidents which enabled the Commons to secure so great a power amid such complete subjection, have been shrewdly suggested by English commentators on parliamentary history. Hatsell points out the consideration that it was important to Henry that he should appear to the Catholic powers of the Continent to have a good understanding with his Parliament. Of course he was ready to do, for such a purpose, anything that did not interfere with his own aims, or involve a material sacrifice of power; and this concession appeared to involve none. He saw in the occasion an opportunity to gain at least as much as he conceded. There had been no doubt that privilege exempted the servants of members, as well as members themselves, from imprisonment; and Henry proposed to share this protection for *his* servants, by reminding them that he also was a part of the Parliament, attending in person upon its sittings. And, as Hatsell suggests, it was quite as much to the fact that Ferrers was his servant, as to the fact that he was their member, that the Commons were indebted for his ready acquiescence in their proceedings. (a) What might have befallen in a case less agreeable to his temper, we have no means of knowing; for *Creketoste's* case, which was the next instance, occurred in the reign of his successor.

We are not to suppose, however, that their jurisdiction, or the application of their privileges, had taken a definite form even in their own minds. They conducted themselves as men always do in the process of acquiring a power. In 1555, when one of their members "was bound in a recognizance in the Star Chamber, to appear before the Council within twelve days after the end of this Parliament," they laid before the Lords a declaration that their privilege was violated thereby. The Lords decided, however, that it was not. 1 Hatsell, 74. They did not under-

---

(a) Mr. Holroyd, in the argument of *Burdett* vs. *Abbott*, said of *Ferrers'* case: "It appears that the allowance of the privilege in that case was as well in respect of the claim of the King for his servants, as of the claim of the House for its members."

take to decide the matter for themselves. And in 1575, when a servant of Mr. Hall, one of their members, was imprisoned for a debt, a committee, to whom they referred the matter, actually reported to the House that they could find no precedent for delivering him by the mace, and that a writ from the Lord Keeper would be necessary. The House accordingly instructed Mr. Hall to apply for a writ of privilege. Some time afterwards (the writ probably not having been granted) they summoned the Sergeants of London, who held the prisoner, and delivered him by their own order. 1 Hatsell, 89. Nothing could better illustrate that this jurisdiction was still in process of formation and establishment.

In the very next case, they assumed the air and power of a court of justice; still swinging between extremes in the manner that is characteristic of an unsettled jurisdiction. In 1580, they arraigned Arthur Hall, one of their members, for having written and published a book which contained what they held to be libelous charges against their House; and the Speaker delivered to him a judgment by which he was condemned to expulsion, to imprisonment for the definite period of six months, and to pay a fine to the Queen. Hatsell speaks of this as a "very new and extraordinary proceeding," and suggests that there must have been a secret history in the case, and that it must have involved some particular offence to the Queen. 1 Hatsell, 93. Very clearly, the proceeding was new and extraordinary, and it shows that the jurisdiction of the House of Commons to inflict punishments depended upon its temper, and had not yet come to have definite limits.

No such extent of power has been exercised in more constitutional times.

The manner in which this jurisdiction of the Commons was exercised during the first forty years of its existence, has already shown that it was brought into existence and moulded by circumstances peculiar to English history; and that it did not accrue to that body because it must belong to every legislative assembly.

But this law of its origin and operation cannot be fully appreciated until we shall have considered the later experiences of the House of Commons. When they first undertook to exercise this power, they made no pretension to determine what their privileges were; they vindicated only such as were universally conceded. But they came in time to claim a right to define as well as to defend their privileges; and we shall find that, throughout their whole course, they were always impelled by the necessities of their peculiar surroundings. Their later history will explain the origin of their peculiar power even better than its beginning has done; because it illustrates the method and law of its existence and growth. We shall find that privileges, inherent in the strictest sense in legislative bodies, would have been lost, but for the assertion of a still larger independence. None of them, for example, could be more indispensable than freedom of speech; and for exercising that right, the Commons were lectured and threatened and punished through still another century. Elizabeth treated that "liberty" as a mere concession of the crown, a sufferance, and not as a constitutional right, equal to her own prerogatives. In her very first Parliament, when the Speaker mentioned freedom of speech, in petitioning for the *ancient* privileges of the Commons, she gave them to understand that it was to be used "reverently and decently;" D'Ewes, 16; 1 Hatsell, 75; and she decided more than once whether it had been so used. Thirty-four years afterwards she caused her Lord Keeper, Sir John Puckering, who had himself been Speaker, to say to them: "Liberty of speech is granted you; but you must know what privilege you have—not to speak every one what he listeth, or what cometh in to his brain to utter—but your privilege is Aye or No." 1 Parl. His. 861; May, 114. It is pretty clear, therefore, that her notion of their privileges was a settled political doctrine of the crown.

On the other hand, she informed them that some matters were not subjects of legislation at all. In these she did not recognize even the privilege of Aye and No. There could be no doubt of their constitutional right to consider measures to prevent a disputed succession; even Henry VIII had employed them in "settling" the crown; but in 1566, while they were discussing the question of her marriage and the succession, she "commanded" them not to proceed further in the matter. They knew she had no right to do so; but even Peter Wentworth, their boldest member, ventured only to doubt whether such an interference was not an infringement of their privileges and liberties. In 1585 she sent for Mr. Speaker Puckering and reprimanded him for allowing a bill to be introduced for the further reform of the church. He communicated her displeasure to the House, and the bill was allowed to drop. 1 Parl. His. 830. In the opening of the next Parliament there came a special order from her, "that no laws should be made at all in this session," and it was strictly obeyed.

But Elizabeth knew when it was best to yield and when it was safe to persist. For example, after ordering Strickland, the mover of certain bills touching religion, to absent himself from the House and await the orders of her privy council, she quietly allowed him to return to his seat, on perceiving the temper of the Commons. But eight years later (1593), when Wentworth and three other members had been sent to prison for petitioning the Lord Keeper that the Lords would join in supplicating her majesty to agree to settle the succession to the crown, she answered a motion for their release by telling the Commons that she had committed them "for causes best known to herself, and that she would release them whenever she thought proper, and would be better pleased to do it of her own proper motion than from their suggestion." D'Ewes, 497.

It is true that in this instance the offenders had not acted in their capacity of members, and their petition to the Lord Keeper was not in the course of legislation. The Commons might still have claimed that their members were not liable to imprisonment for such a matter, but their ground was not so strong as in Strickland's case, and they submitted. It is clear enough that parliamentary privilege was not established yet.

Their worst experiences, however, were to come. Elizabeth had no inclination to degrade the manhood of her people, and found no pleasure in the mere humiliation of their representatives. She rarely touched their privileges, till they touched the twin subjects of her jealousy—marriage and supremacy; and more than once, after a sharp beginning, her good sense persuaded her to desist. But her successor, who had no sense, detested manhood as an insult to himself, and regarded the humiliation of the Commons as their proper and desirable condition. Accordingly his violations of their right of free speech were limited only by his personal cowardice. Had he been as brave as Elizabeth, "privilege" would have become extinct, and Parliaments would have ceased.

The struggle of the Commons with this dynasty of insolence and stupidity and falsehood was thoroughly dramatic. It was by situations that the necessity was developed and the argument was furnished, for an independence which should in all respects and by every instrumentality, take care of its own interests.

Throughout this struggle there was no uncertainty about their rights; there was simply insecurity for want of remedies. In his very first Parliament, 1604, they informed James that their privileges and liberties were their right and due inheritance, no less than their lands and goods; and could not be withheld, denied, or impaired, but with apparent wrong to the whole estate of the realm; and they explained to him that their making request, in the entrance of Parliament, to enjoy their privileges, was an act of manners, and weakened their right no more than their suing to the King for their lands by petition. 1 Hatsell, 227. But James was not afraid of talk—he could out-talk any man in the kingdom—and that was all the Commons had got to yet. So he berated them roundly for their speeches, and, three years after their famous Apology, they fell back to a position in which rights and accountability were about equally mingled. They made known to him, through their Speaker, their earnest desire that he would listen to no private reports of their doings, but take his information of the House's meaning from themselves; that he would be pleased to allow such members as he had blamed to clear themselves in his hearing, and that he would, by some gracious message, let them know that they might deliver their opinions in their places without restraint or fear! (Macfarlane's Eng. B. 7, C. 1.) Certainty of right and uncertainty of tenure could not well come into sharper antithesis than in this prayer.

They had ample reason for their uncertainty of tenure. In 1614, at the close of what was called the Addle Parliament, because it did not pass a single bill, James sent five of their members to the Tower for "licentiousness of speech." Meantime it is some relief to reflect that this very Parliament, by refusing to pass any bill until their grievances should be redressed, had done a great deal towards the establishment of its rights. When the King dissolved them, they had made as long a step for independence as he appeared to have done for despotism.

It was a good while before the direct contest was renewed; for James kept out of their way by not having any Parliament for the next six years; but at last he had to come back to subsidies, and they were confronted once more in the famous Parliament of 1621. During a five months recess of that Parliament, several eminent persons, and among them Sir Edwin Sandys, "a bold-spoken member of the Lower

House," were arbitrarily arrested. The Commons knew well enough that these proceedings had been provoked by the expression of liberal opinions, and they stood by their member. As no prosecution had been instituted against him, the way was open. Sandys was sick in bed; so they sent two members to wait upon him and hear from his own mouth the cause of his arrest. The King, hearing that they were about to take this step, wrote to the Speaker that it was not for anything done in Parliament, and then he added: "but to put them out of doubt of any question of that nature that may arise among them hereafter, you shall resolve them in our name, that we think ourselves very free and able to punish any man's misdemeanors in Parliament, as well during their sitting as after; which we mean not to spare hereafter, upon any occasion of any man's insolent behavior there, that shall be ministered unto us." 1 Hatsell, 137. The House answered by a remonstrance, asserting their undoubted right of free speech as an inheritance from their ancestors. To that the King replied from Newmarket, saying of their privilege " We could not allow of the style, calling it their ancient and undoubted right and inheritance, but could rather have wished that they had said, their privileges were derived from the grace and permission of our ancestors and us ; for most of them grow from precedents, which showeth rather a toleration than an inheritance. The plain truth is, we cannot with patience endure our subjects to use such anti-monarchial words to us, concerning their liberties, except that they had subjoined that they were granted to them by the grace and power of our predecessors."

He added, that, so long as they contained themselves within the limits of their duty, he would be as careful of their privileges as of his own prerogative, so that they never touched on that prerogative, which would enforce him or any just King to retrench their privileges.

The issue was now made up: the King asserted that the privileges of Parliament existed only by his sufferance, and depended entirely on what he might consider their good behavior: the Commons, that they owned their privileges as much as they owned their lands. It was a hot question and the House was so thoroughly exasperated that the King took fright. His courtiers in that body tried to apologize for these expressions as a slip of the pen, and James wrote a letter to Secretary Calvert to qualify what he had said. But even in that letter, he could not abstain from re-asserting that the liberties and privileges of the House were not of undoubted right and inheritance, unless they were so from being granted by the grace and favor of his predecessors on the throne.

The temper which these stupendous pretensions aroused may be imagined from the fact that a committee of the whole house was appointed to meet next day, when, with the help of Sir Edward Coke, Mr. Noy and Mr. Glanville, they drew up the following Protestation: "The Commons now assembled in Parliament, being justly occasioned thereunto, concerning sundry liberties, franchises, privileges, and jurisdictions of Parliament, amongst others not herein mentioned, do make this protestation following:— That the liberties, franchises, privileges, and jurisdictions of Parliament are the ancient and undoubted birthright and inheritance of the Subjects of England; and that the arduous and urgent affairs concerning the King's state, and the defence of the realm, and of the Church of England, and the making and maintenance of laws, and redress of mischiefs and grievances, which daily happen within this realm, are proper subjects and matter of counsel and debate in Parliament; and that, in the handling and proceeding of those businesses, every member of the House hath, and of right ought to have, freedom of speech to propound, treat, reason, and bring to conclusion the same: that the Commons in Parliament have like liberty and freedom to treat of those matters in such order as, in their judgment, shall seem fittest; and that every such member of the said House hath like freedom from all impeachment, imprisonment, and molestation (other than by the censure of the House itself) for or concerning any bill, speaking, reasoning or declaring of any matter or matters touching the Parliament or Parliament business; and that, if any of the said members be complained of and questioned for anything said or done in Parliament, the same is to be shown to the King by the advice and assent of all the Commons assembled in Parliament, before the King give credence to any private information." After a debate which lasted until the then unusual hour of five or six in the evening, the Commons entered this Protestation upon their journal "as of record."

This was intolerable insolence, and James' wrath overcame his cowardice. He rode up to London foaming at the mouth, prorogued Parliament, ordered the clerk of the House of Commons to bring him the

Journal Book, and with his own hand tore out the Protestation. Then in his council-book he caused to be entered this: "His Majesty did, in full assembly of his council, and in the presence of the judges, declare the said protestation to be invalid, annulled, void, and of no effect." If negativing words could make it naught, the protestation was annihilated. A few days afterwards he closed their mouths effectually by an insulting proclamation of dissolution. 1 Hatsell, 137; Macfarlane's Eng. B. 7, anno 1621; and then he sent Coke and Sir Robert Phillips and Mr. Seldon to prison. He could refute the doctrine of free speech in that way, if in no other.

But trouble always disturbed his theory of divine power. Three years later, when he was deeply in debt, when the Spanish marriage had miscarried, when everything had gone wrong, he addressed his last Parliament in a tone of moderation and sweetness. He told them that he remembered and regretted past misunderstandings; that he hoped they would judge him charitably, as they wished to be judged, and that he earnestly desired to do his duty and manifest his love to his people. In plain English, he wanted money dreadfully.

But this lull in the contest meant nothing; or rather it only meant that freedom was to come by contest. The Stewart devil was a monk only while he was sick. And there were other Stewarts. James died in the next year, but he only made room for a more serious and determined fool, a fool on principle.

Charles went to work promptly and kept on industriously. Immediately after his coronation, when the Commons were getting ready to impeach Buckingham, he said to them: "I must let you know that I will not allow any of my servants to be questioned amongst you, much less such as are of eminent place and near unto me." The Commons replied that it was "the ancient, constant and undoubted right and usage of Parliaments to question and complain of all persons, of what degree soever, found dangerous to the commonwealth in abusing the power and trust committed to them by the Sovereign."

They went on with their impeachment and presented their articles to the Lords. Two days afterwards Sir John Eliot and Sir Dudley Digges, two of their managers who had been especially severe in their denunciations, were called out of the House, as if the King had sent for them, and were carried by water to the Tower. It was given out that their arrest was for high treason, but Charles explained to the House of Lords: "I have thought fit to punish some insolent speeches lately spoken. I have been too remiss hitherto in punishing such speeches as concern myself." The Commons debated this violation of their privileges with closed doors, and came to a resolution to stay all business till satisfaction was given. Courage and a cool head triumphed; Eliot and Digges returned to their seats in the House. Nevertheless the King stopped their impeachment by dissolving Parliament. He had been little more than a year on the throne, and had already defeated a constitutional power and violated the most essential privilege of the House of Commons.

In that same session he had told them to remember that Parliaments were altogether in his power for their calling, sitting, or dissolution; and that therefore, as he should find the fruits of them good or evil, they were to be or not to be. But in less than two years Buckingham's disastrous expedition into France, and the want of money, compelled him to confront the most respectable House of Commons that had ever convened. The "fruit" this time was the famous Petition of Right. He tried to cheat them by a pretended assent, then assented squarely, and then explained it away. Finally he prorogued the Parliament for some months, and of course violated that statute in the meantime.

When they came together, after another prorogation, in 1629, the Commons would talk of nothing but religion, illegal taxes, and arbitrary imprisonments. The King insisted that they should talk first of his subsidies, and finding that they would not, adjourned them for a few days by his peremptory command. It was his prerogative to dissolve and prorogue Parliaments, but it was their privilege, so long as a session continued at all, to fix their own adjournments. Nevertheless they quietly obeyed. A few weeks later he tried that device again, and then they understood themselves better. In the midst of a debate Mr. Speaker Finch announced to them a message commanding him "to adjourn the House until Tuesday come seven-night following;" but they kept their seats, saying they had somewhat to finish. Eliot produced a remonstrance against the illegal laying of tonnage and poundage, which he desired the Speaker to read. Finch pleaded that the King had adjourned the House. The clerk was called on, and he too refused. Then Eliot read it himself and demanded the question. The Speaker only repeated the King's command, and proceeded to rise. But the English blood was up now, and Hollis, Valentine, and other members of that stamp, held him in his chair; some of the patriots at the same time locking the doors and bringing the keys up to the table. The courtiers rushed to release the pinioned Speaker, but they were too weak, and poor Finch sat still at last, actually weeping, and crying that he dared not put the question because he had the King's commands. Of course it was impossible to make him do it, and, knowing it was their last opportunity to express their sentiments, they hastily drew up a protest. While Hollis was reading it amid the cheers of the House, the King had hurried down to the House of Lords, expecting to find the Commons adjourned. Not seeing the Speaker, he sent a messenger to bring away the Sergeant with his mace. That would have adjourned the House; but the members stopped the Sergeant and took from him the keys of the doors. Then the King, seeing no Sergeant, dispatched the Usher of the Black Rod to call up the Commons for a dissolution; but the Commons would not let the Usher in. Charles sent for the Captain of the Pensioners and his guards, and ordered them to force the door—but they came too late. The Commons had voted their protest, had adjourned themselves to the tenth of March, and were gone.

When they met again, the King made an end of that Parliament without even inviting the Commons to the ceremony of dissolution; telling the Lords, in his speech, that the offending members were *vipers*, who must look for their rewards.

He kept his word better this time than he had

done about the Petition of Right. Eliot, Hollis, Selden, Valentine, Coriton, Hobart, Hayman, Long, and Stroud, the members who had been active in getting up the protest and keeping the Speaker in his chair, were summoned before the privy-council and sent to the Tower.

Charles was determined to proceed against them in the Star Chamber, and Lord Keeper Coventry set about preparing the way for him by drawing an opinion from the Judges. Those learned persons were complacent enough to say, "that freedom of speech only extends to things debated in Parliament *in a parliamentary course*, and that a Parliament man, committing an offence against the King or council in Parliament, not in a Parliament way, may be punished for it after the Parliament ended; for the Parliament shall not give privilege to any one *contra morem parliamentarium* exceeding the bounds of his place and duty." 2 Lives of the Chanc. 535; 1 Lives of the Ch. Just. 385. And to meet the special case, they added, that, "by false slanders to bring the Lords of the council and the judges, not in a parliamentary way, into the hatred of the people, and the Government into contempt, was punishable, out of Parliament, *in the Star Chamber*, as an offence committed in Parliament beyond the office, and beside the duty of a Parliament man." 2 Lives of the Ch. Just. 385.

The imprisoned members sued for their writs of habeas corpus, and were brought before the King's Bench. The Judges had come to the opinion that they were entitled to bail, but the King sent for them and commanded them to deliver no opinion until they should have consulted the other Judges; and so, by

quibbles and dodges, the matter was held undecided
for that term, and the prisoners were kept in close
custody during the whole of the long vacation which
ensued.

Toward the end of the vacation Chief Justice Hyde
and Judge Whitelock were sent by the Lord Keeper
down to Hampton Court. The King told them he
was willing the imprisoned members should be admitted to bail, notwithstanding their contumacy in
refusing to declare that they were sorry for having
offended him; and that he should abandon the Star
Chamber proceedings and prosecute them in the
King's Bench. On the first day of Michaelmas Term
they were brought into court, and ordered, not only
to find bail for the present charge, but sureties for
their good behavior in future. Of course they refused
to give sureties, but were ready with bail for their
appearance. Thereupon they were all sent back to
the Tower.

Then came the prosecution. The Attorney General
filed an ex-officio information in the King's Bench
against Sir John Eliot, Mr. Hollis and Mr. Valentine.
Eliot was charged with words uttered in the Commons' House, and particularly with saying "that the
privy council and judges had conspired to trample
under foot the liberties of the subject." Hollis and
Valentine were charged with the tumult on the last
day of the session, when Speaker Finch was held in
his chair. The defendants pleaded to the jurisdiction
of the court: "Forasmuch as these offences are supposed to have been done in Parliament, they ought
not to be punished in this court, or any other except
in Parliament." Without waiting to hear counsel,

Chief Justice Hyde at once said, "that all the Judges had already resolved with one voice, that an offence committed in Parliament, criminally or contemptuously, the Parliament being ended, rests punishable in the Court of King's Bench, in which the King by intendment sitteth." Counsel for the defendants insisted on being heard, but they might as well have been silent. Hyde treated their arguments with scorn, and concluded by observing: "As to what was said, that an inferior court cannot meddle with matters done in a superior, true it is that an inferior court cannot meddle with the *judgments* of a superior court; but if particular members of a superior court offend, they are oft-times punishable in an inferior—as if a judge shall commit a capital offence in this court he may be arraigned thereof at Newgate. The behavior of Parliament men ought to be parliamentary. Parliament is a higher court than this, but every member of Parliament is not a court, and if he commit an offence we may punish him. The information charges that the defendants acted unlawfully, and they could have no privilege to violate the law. No outrageous speeches have been made against a great minister of state in Parliament that have not been punished." 1 Lives Ch. Just. 386. The court overruled the plea to its jurisdiction, and the prisoners refused to put in any other. On the last day of the next term judgment was given against them upon *nihil dicit*. Mr. Justice Jones assured them that, heavy as was their offence, their punishment should be laid on "with a light hand;" and then he delivered the following sentence: 1. That every of the defendants shall be imprisoned during the King's pleasure.

Sir John Eliot to be imprisoned in the Tower of London, and the other defendants in other prisons. 2. That none of them shall be delivered out of prison until he give security in this court for his good behavior, and have made submission and acknowledgment of his offence. 3. Sir John Eliot, inasmuch as we think him the greatest offender, and the ringleader, shall pay to the King a fine of 2000*l.*, and Mr. Hollis a fine of 1000 marks; and Mr. Valentine, because he is of less ability than the rest, shall pay a fine of 500*l.*" Macfarlane's Eng. B. 7. (1629.)

All of the defendants except Sir John Eliot were liberated on bail, after a detention of eighteen months. When he had lain four years in the Tower, his health began to decline rapidly, and his friends prevailed upon him to petition the King. Charles' only answer to that petition was: "It is not humble enough." Then he sent another by his son, expressing his hearty sorrow for having displeased his majesty, and humbly beseeching him once again to command the judges to set him at liberty; and when he had recovered his health he might return back to his prison, there to undergo such punishment as God had allotted him. The lieutenant of the Tower took offence at his sending the petition by another hand than his; but offered to deliver another for him, if he would humble himself before his majesty, acknowledging his fault. Eliot, thanking him for his friendly advice, replied that his spirits had grown feeble and faint; that when he recovered his former vigor he would think about it. And so, as brave on a sick bed as other men upon their feet, he died, a prisoner in the Tower, on the 27th of November, 1632.

For eleven long years of illegality and torture and swindling misgovernment, the voice of Parliament was not heard again. But when they came together in 1640 they had good memories. On the second day of the session, Pym delivered a speech in which he said: "The first of grievances are those which, during this interval of eleven years, have been directed against the liberties and privileges of Parliament;" and on the following day the House voted that the proceedings remaining upon record in the King's Bench and Court of Star Chamber against Sir John Eliot, Mr. Hollis, and the other imprisoned members of the Parliament of 1628, should be sent for and referred to a committee. Two days afterwards they resolved that the conduct of Mr. Speaker Finch, in that Parliament, in not obeying the commands of the House, and his adjournment by command of the King, were breaches of privilege. They persisted in talking about grievances before they would talk about money; and the swift end of it was a dissolution after a fruitless session of about three weeks.

That amazing person, his Majesty, was blind to the fast quickening current and deaf to the cataract below. As if the imprisonment of members for words spoken in their own House had not made bad blood enough; as if Eliot had been forgotten—he committed several members the very day after the dissolution. Their speeches and official action in Parliament were the only offences charged against them. Finally, in 1642, he reached his climax, in attempting to bring Hollis, Hazelrig, Pym, Hampden, and Strode, the five leaders of the Commons, before the House of Lords, to be tried on a trumped up charge of levying war against him. A broken promise, a fiction, a lie of some sort, was almost his sole device. Finding the Lords troubled with doubts, he went himself to the Commons' House, attended by his gentlemen-pensioners, and followed by hundreds of courtiers, officers, and soldiers of fortune, most of them armed with swords and pistols, to seize the five members in their seats. But they were gone. Next day the Commons removed to the City and sat in Guildhall. On the day following, accompanied this time only by his usual attendants, the King sought them there.

As he rode through the streets, he was saluted with cries of "privileges of Parliament, privileges of Parliament," and at the door of Guildhall he was confronted by the Common Council, who had assembled as friends of the Commons. To these gentlemen he dropped his haughty tone, but he demanded their assistance in bringing him the five members. He went back without them, and then by proclamation he commanded the magistrates to apprehend and carry them to the Tower. London answered by an offer of her sailors and famous apprentices to escort the Commons safely back to Westminster, and they returned in a triumphant procession of boats, watched by their troops along the shore. The King had left London the day before, not to return till he came as a prisoner. Rushworth, Vol. 4, p. 474.

But the Commons were not done yet with the invasion of their privileges. They impeached Mr. Attorney General Herbert, by whom the accusation against their members had been presented to the Lords. The gist of his offence was "a breach of privilege," and the fact that he acted by express command of the King did not save him. The sentence of the Lords was: "That he was disabled and made incapable of being a member, assistant or pleader in either house of Parliament, * * and that he should be committed forthwith to the Fleet."

Just a hundred years ago, the Commons had secured the King's assent to their proceedings in punishing an act which, he was careful to say, touched his dignity as well as their own. By suffering and outrage, they had reached a point when an attack upon their privileges by the King himself could be punished in the person of his instrument. Power had been forced upon them by denial of their rights.

Need any further evidence be offered, to prove that it was only the necessity of *circumstances*, of a situation peculiar to that legislative body, which brought about the concession of an independent jurisdiction to protect their own privileges, and afterwards drove the Commons to enlarge that jurisdiction? Is there any room to doubt that it was conceded substantially because the law of the realm, the Constitution, had failed to provide, and in the end was unable to provide, any of the means to protect them against the obstructions to which they were exposed? Or that they were forced to enlarge it, because notwithstanding its first extent, their privileges were not merely unprotected but actively assailed by the co-existing powers of the State?

When liberty of speech was denied by the sovereign, and punished as a crime by the Courts; when their personal liberty was violated by arbitrary arrests, and the judges dared not bail them without the consent of their master; when even these intimidated tribunals were put aside, and in order to make sure work, their members were tried by an unconstitutional court which cared still less for law—it became simply a question of existence. In all England no voice but their own was ready to affirm their rights, no arm but their own would move to protect them. Amid such antagonisms it was absolutely inevitable that they should undertake to determine for themselves when their privileges were invaded; and this necessity settled all the consequences.

It compelled a choice, whether to be a defenceless party before other tribunals, or to be themselves a tribunal. Not that they could take the attitude of a tribunal towards the power whose conduct had produced the necessity; but when the claim to judge of their own privileges was once made, it followed that, although they could only argue and protest to the Sovereign, they must, in all other directions where they had power to do so, insist upon submission to their judgment. Power to punish violations of privileges so adjudged, was part of the position into which they were forced. (a)

(a) Lord Campbell, who at all times sturdily maintained the power of the House of Commons to punish for contempts, did not see fit to claim for it an inherent necessity. When he was Attorney General he described its true ground in the following words: "Privilege is given to the House of Commons to be exercised against the Crown and the House of Lords; unless the Commons were themselves the tribunal by which their privilege is to be judged, it would have been abolished long ago. The necessity of preserving it from interference by the Courts of Law is not to be estimated from the present improved state of the courts. The law of privilege was settled when Judges were the creatures of the Crown, and liable to be discarded if not obedient, and when the Kings themselves used to interfere in the administration of justice; which they did personally and as judges in ancient times, and afterwards by letters to the judges, directing them how to act in particular cases; a practice

If it be true, then, that this power of the Commons to adjudicate their own rights and punish their own wrongs was conceded to them, effectively, in order to supply a defect of the Constitution, and grew by reason of its violations, what becomes of the argument that a similar judicature is necessarily incident to the existence of every supreme legislative assembly? What is there in this example, which has always been held up to us, which proves that such a power is congenital and inherent in all such bodies? Is it the fact that the Commons lived nearly three centuries without possessing it? It became necessary to that body because the Constitution which established it could not furnish it any other assured protection; is it to be implied that it belongs to legislative bodies established by a Constitution which is careful at the same time to authorize perfectly assured and absolutely sufficient means by which they could be protected? Is it seriously contended that a power which accrued by reason of a scramble for life among the forces of the State in England, is essential to the existence of legislative bodies under a Constitution which forbids such a contest by defining the limits of authority and rendering encroachments impossible? It was not according to the methods of the common law to act upon or affirm

---

several times checked by Statute, as, in particular, by Stat. 2 Edw. 3, c. 8, and 18 Edw. 3, c. 4. And although the judges are now independent of the Crown, there may still be a proper constitutional jealousy lest, at some time, a desire of popularity, or of extending the jurisdiction of the Courts, should lead them to decisions against wholesome and useful privilege, as mischievous as those formerly given in submission to the King's authority. But during the struggles of the House of Commons against the Crown, as in the reigns of Elizabeth, James I, and Charles I, the privileges of the House would clearly not have survived, if they had depended on the ruling of judges." Argument in *Stockdale* vs. *Hansard*, 9 Adol. & Ell. 29.

any general principle in giving this power to the House of Commons; in granting jurisdictions and powers, that law never pretended to do anything more than meet the exigencies of English life; but if this particular grant is susceptible of any generalization, it is only to this extent: When the constitution under which a legislative assembly exists, refuses or fails to provide for its protection by authorizing adequate means of punishing its wrongdoers; *a fortiori*, when such an assembly is compelled to struggle for existence against the other powers of the State, it then becomes necessary, not only in fact but in contemplation of law, that it shall take into its own hands the means of protection by punishment.

In attributing common-law powers to institutions in this country, the method of argument has been, that the powers of English common-law institutions belong, by an implication of necessity, to institutions of a similar character and similarly situated here. Even according to this theory, it will be time enough to make the implication when the similar situation occurs.

With sincere deference to the great authorities who have so long argued from this premise, it is submitted that any reference to the political necessities of the time of the Tudors and the Stewarts, is only a delusive anachronism. The impropriety of insisting that obsolete necessity is inherent and vital, has been indicated to us by the very body which first asserted it, and in connection with this very matter of privilege. In the time of James I, no privilege was more essential to the independence of the House of Commons, than its function of determining all questions touching the elections and returns of its members;

yet, in the time of Victoria, at the instance of that House, jurisdiction to determine controverted elections has been substantially turned over to the Courts of Justice. By the "Elections Petitions and Corrupt Practices at Elections" Act of 1868, the trial of such questions in England was confided to the Court of Common Pleas at Westminster; in Ireland, to the Court of Common Pleas, at Dublin; and in Scotland, to the Court of Sessions. By this Act they declared that it was not essential that they should themselves apply the remedies, even in a matter which affected their composition.

And by another Act, passed almost exactly a century earlier, Parliament had revised and overruled the ancient opinion as to the very amount of protection which was necessary to its members. From the earliest days, it had been a part of a member's protection that his domestics should be included in the privilege from arrest; and if usage could be said to establish a conclusion of law as to what was necessary, it had done so in this matter, quite as much as in respect to the manner in which the personal privilege of the member himself, or the common privilege of the assembly, should be protected. Yet, by the Act of 10 Geo. 3, ch. 50, the privilege from arrest was taken away from members' servants.

We have thus far referred only to historical materials. Let us inquire next how the question, whether this power accrued by legal necessity, has been treated by the judicial authorities.

Probably, the notion that it was based upon an *inherent* necessity, of which the law must take notice, was not unfamiliar, even before its announcement by Lord Ellenborough. Chief Justice De Grey so characterized it in 1771, in *Brass Crosby's* case. 3 Wilson, 188. But it was Lord Ellenborough who first gave to it judicial standing. In *Burdett* vs. *Abbott* he said: "The mere power of removing actual impediments to its proceedings would not be sufficient for the purposes of its full and efficient protection. It must also have the power of protecting itself from insult and indignity wherever offered, by punishing those who offer it. * * And would it consist with the dignity of such bodies, or what is more, with the immediate and effectual exercise of their important functions, that they should wait the comparatively tardy result of a prosecution in the ordinary courts of law, for the vindication of their privileges from wrong and insult? The necessity of the case would therefore, upon principles of natural reason, seem to require that *such bodies, constituted for such purposes, and exercising such functions as they do*, should possess the powers which the history of the earliest times shows they have in fact possessed and used."

It is amazing that so eminent a judge should so ignore the plain facts of constitutional history, and confound a necessity which was produced by circumstances, with inherent necessity. After he had proven that this power of the Commons was established by usage, and affirmed by statute,—he might have said it began by what was equal to a statute—such speculations upon its origin were uncalled for; and, as they were nothing more than speculations, they should have had no influence over later decisions. They laid down a proposition, however, which habit and reverence made acceptable, and they did have influence in a tribunal where this question of origin was not irrelevant, but must be considered.

Burdett vs. *Abbott* was supposed to have demonstrated that every supreme legislature, established where the common law of England was in force, was invested with power to punish contempts offered to it, on the ground, that such power was a necessary legal incident to its functions. Accordingly, in 1836, the Judicial Committee of the Privy Council held, in the case of *Beaumont* vs. *Barrett*, 1 Moore's Privy Council Cases, 59, that the House of Assembly of Jamaica, being the supreme legislative assembly of that island, had that power.

The appellant had been committed, on the Speaker's warrant, for a breach of the privileges of the House in publishing certain paragraphs in a newspaper. Baron Parke, delivering the opinion of the Committee, said: "It would appear, I think, to be inherent in every legislative assembly that possesses a supreme legislative authority, to have the power of punishing contempts; and not merely such as are a direct obstruction to its due course of proceeding, but such also as have a tendency indirectly to produce such an obstruction; in the same way as the Courts of record may not only remove or punish persons who actually are interrupting their functions, but may also repress those who indirectly impede the administration of Justice by disparaging or weakening their authority."

This decision was the first fruit of Lord Ellenborough's *dictum;* and it is noteworthy as an example of the mischief that may be done by uncalled for judicial speculations.

Five years later, a similar question came before the Judicial Committee of the Privy Council, in the case of *Kielley* vs. *Carson* and others, 4 Moore's Privy Council Cases, 63, when the same learned judge, referring to the earlier decision of the Committee in *Beaumont* vs. *Barrett*, said: "Their Lordships do not consider that case as one by which they ought to be bound in deciding the present question. The opinion of their Lordships, delivered by myself immediately after the argument closed, though it clearly expressed that the power was incidental to every Legislative Assembly, was not the only ground on which that judgment rested, and, therefore, was in some degree extra-judicial; but, besides, it was stated to be, and was, founded entirely on the dictum of Lord Ellenborough in *Burdett* vs. *Abbott;* which dictum we all think cannot be taken as an authority for the abstract proposition, that every legislative assembly has the power of committing for contempts."

The case of *Kielley* vs. *Carson*, which, notwithstanding the slight reservation that *Beaumont* vs. *Barrett* went also on another ground, overruled that decision, was, on account of the importance of this question, ordered to a second argument, and was then heard by a committee which included Lyndhurst, Lord Chancellor; Denman, Chief Justice of Queen's Bench; Abinger, Chief Baron of the Exchequer; Cottenham, late Lord Chancellor; Campbell, Chancellor of the Duchy of Lancaster; Shadwell, Vice-Chancellor; Erskine, Justice of Common Pleas; Parke, Baron of the Exchequer, and Dr. Lushington,

Judge of the Admiralty Court. Certainly it must be accepted as a well considered case, and of the highest authority. Baron Parke, in delivering the opinion of the Committee, said: "The main question raised by the pleadings was, whether the House of Assembly [of New Foundland] had the power to arrest and bring before them, with a view to punishment, a person charged by one of its members with having used insolent language to him, out of the doors of the House, in reference to his conduct as a member of the Assembly—in other words, whether the House had the power, such as is possessed by both Houses of Parliament in England, to adjudicate upon a contempt or breach of privilege.

"Their Lordships are of opinion, that the House of Assembly do not possess the power of arrest, with a view to adjudication on a complaint of contempt committed out of its doors.

"Their Lordships see no reason to think, that in the principle of the common law, any other powers are given them [the local legislatures] than such as are necessary to the existence of such a body, and the proper exercise of the functions which it is intended to execute. These powers are granted by the very act of its establishment; an act which on both sides it is admitted, it was competent for the Crown to perform. This is the principle which governs all legal incidents: *Quando lex aliquid concedit, concedere videtur et illud, sine quo res ipsa esse non potest.* In conformity to this principle we feel no doubt that such an assembly has the right of protecting itself from all impediments to the due course of its proceedings. To the full extent of every measure which it may be really necessary to adopt, to secure the free exercise of their legislative functions, they are justified in acting, by the principle of the common law. But the power of punishing any past misconduct, as a contempt of its authority, and adjudicating upon the fact of such contempt and the measure of punishment, as a judicial body, irresponsible to the party accused, whatever the real facts may be, is of a very different character, and by no means essentially necessary for the exercise of its functions by a local legislature, whether representative or not. All these functions may be well performed without this extraordinary power, and with the aid of the ordinary tribunals to investigate and punish contemptuous insults and interruptions."

In 1866, the question, whether a grant of legislative power included a grant of power to punish for contempts, came again before the Privy Council, in the case of *Doyle* vs. *Falconer*, Law Rep. 1 Privy Council Cases, 328; and this time it came in a shape which would have secured an affirmative answer, if such an answer could be given in any case whatever.

A member of the Lower House of Assembly of Dominica, having been guilty of disorderly and contemptuous conduct in the course of debate and *in the face of the House*, was committed upon the Speaker's warrant, for contempt. The case at bar was an action for trespass and false imprisonment.

After discussing the proposition, that the Assembly had the power of commitment, because its functions were analogous to those of the House of Commons, which possessed that power, Sir James Colville, delivering the opinion of the Committee, said: "If, then, the power assumed by the House of Assembly cannot be maintained by analogy to the privileges of the House of Commons, or the powers of a court of record, is there any other legal foundation on which it may be rested? It has not, as both sides admit, been expressly granted. The learned counsel for the appellant invoked the principle of the common law; and, as it must be conceded that the common law sanctions the exercise of the prerogative by which the Assembly has been created, the principle of the common law, which is embodied in its maxim *Quando lex aliquid concedit, concedere videtur et illud, sine quo res ipsa esse non potest,* applies to the body so created. The question, therefore, is reduced to this: Is the power to punish and commit for contempts committed in its presence, one necessary to the existence of such a body as the Assembly of Dominica, and the proper exercise of the functions which it is intended to execute? It is necessary to distinguish between a power to punish for a contempt, and a power to remove any obstruction offered to the deliberations or proper action of a legislative body during its sittings; which last power is necessary for self-preservation. If a member of a colonial House of Assembly is guilty of disorderly conduct in the House while sitting, he may be removed or excluded for a time, or even expelled; but there is a great difference between such powers and the judicial power of inflicting a penal sentence for the offence. The right to remove for self-security is one thing; the right to inflict punishment is another. The former is, in their lordships' judgment, all that is warranted by the legal maxim that has been cited, but the latter is not its legitimate consequence."

It is worth while to call attention to the peculiar position of Lord Denman in this matter. Only a year before the decision of *Kielley* vs. *Carson*, he had said, in *Queen* vs. *Gossett*, 3 Perry & Dav., 362: " a deliberative assembly must have the power in itself to vindicate its privileges, which can only be by committing for contempt;" and in the *Sheriff of Middlesex*, 11 Adol. & Ell., 273, he had said: " Representative bodies must necessarily vindicate their authority by means of their own; and those remedies lie in the process of committal for contempt." But he fully concurred with the Committee in *Kielley* vs. *Carson*, where it was said by Baron Parke, that " the reason why the House of Commons has this power is *not because it is a representative body with legislative functions*, but by virtue of ancient usage and prescription; the lex et conseuetudo Parliamenti, which forms a part of the Common Law of the land, and according to which the High Court of Parliament, before its division, and the houses of Lords and Commons, since, are invested with many *peculiar* privileges, that of punishment for contempts being one." When two such judges as Denman and Parke abandon opinions recently announced by them, their later conclusions must be supposed to have been considered with great deliberation. If authority can settle such questions, this circumstance, and the number and eminence of the judges who composed the Judicial Committee in the case of *Kielley* vs. *Carson*, make the decision of that tribunal absolutely conclusive as to the ground on which the jurisdiction of the House of Commons stood.

It is to be observed that these decisions not only deny the general proposition that power to punish contempts is held by the common law to be inherent in legislative assemblies, but they deny the specific proposition that the power exercised by the House of Commons in contemplation of that law, stood upon the principle of self-protection. And it is particularly important to observe that, while Lord Ellenborough's dictum, in *Burdett* vs. *Abbott*, claimed that this power was incident *ex necessitate* and for the purpose of self-protection, the judgment in that case placed it upon a different ground. In justifying the breaking of Burdett's outer door, all of the judges rested the power of the House upon the principle that the proceedings were in prosecution of a public offence. That power to do an act which was justifiable only because it concerned the public interest, could not originate in the special right of *self*-preservation, needs no argument. On its face it is a purely jurisdictional power.

It should now be considered to be settled, therefore, by the highest English authority, that the power of the House of Commons to adjudicate and inflict punishment for contempts was, in the language of Baron Parke, merely one of "many *peculiar* privileges" which belonged to that body; and that it existed by authority of positive law and not *ex necessitate*.

The force of these Privy Council decisions cannot be diminished by alleging that they relate to the powers of colonial, or what the Committee called "local" legislatures. The question under consideration assumed its broadest possible form; it was: What powers does the common law of England understand to be necessarily included in the establishment of a legislative assembly and in a grant of "legislative power?" Of course, in construing such a grant, the dimensions of the grantee cannot be material. There might be subjects about which a local legislature had no authority to legislate at all, just as there are subjects about which the Congress of the United States cannot legislate; but, in both cases, the power actually given is general legislative power. And as to the matter of protection, the necessity of a colonial legislature must be, in contemplation of law, precisely the same as the necessity of independent legislatures. When the functions of a legislative body are those of *government*, affecting the peace, good order, property, safety, and personal liberties of the community which it governs, it must be just as necessary that it should be undisturbed by obstructions of any kind, as if those functions were imperial.

But the consideration of chief importance in the present discussion is, that the Privy Council were called upon to determine what powers the common law of England had concluded to be necessarily comprehended in a grant of *legislative power*, and that they have decided that it had not concluded that power to inflict punishment was so comprehended.

Are we any longer at liberty, then, to insist that the necessity of this power is a conclusion of the common law, and to found implications upon that proposition?

2. We come now to the precedent of the Superior Courts of Justice, which has been relied upon, as establishing a conclusion that the principle of self-protection includes, in the cases of certain bodies, power to secure that protection by punishment.

The meaning of this reference to the courts must be, that such use of the power establishes a conclusion of law that it is necessary to self-protection, not only in that case, but in analogous cases; and that the case of a legislative body is analogous. We have therefore to consider, on what ground this power of the Superior Courts in England originally stood; whether, namely, it accrued to them on the principle of self-protection, or whether they exercised it merely as a *function*, vested in them by the common law just as all their other functions were vested in them, and as a matter of jurisdiction.

Blackstone, whose reasons for the law are apt to be accepted as having the same authority with his statement of the law, has been understood to affirm that the courts took this power incidentally, and because otherwise they could not exercise the functions specially vested in them. After enumerating the contempts which they might punish, he says: " The process of attachments for these and the like contempts must necessarily be as ancient as the laws themselves; for the laws, without a competent authority to secure their administration from disobedience and contempt, would be vain and nugatory. A power, therefore, in the Superior Courts of Justice, to suppress such contempts by an immediate attachment of the offender, results from the first principles of judicial establishments, and must be an inseparable attendant upon every superior tribunal. Accordingly we find it actually exercised as early as the annals of our law extend." 4 Bl. 286.

This is a very strong statement of the necessity that such a power should be vested somewhere; and the learned Commentator very distinctly asserts that it "results from the first principles of Judicial establishments;" and that it should be "an inseparable attendant upon every *superior* tribunal." But this is very far from an assertion that it was an implied *power of self-preservation;* since so accurate a writer could not fail to perceive that, in that case, the power should be an attendant upon inferior, as well as upon superior tribunals. Whether consciously or not, he was only occupied in pointing out that kind of necessity which *induced the grant* of the power; and has affirmed nothing more than that the necessity for "a competent authority," to secure the administration of the laws from disobedience and contempt, required the grant of summary power to the *superior* tribunals. That he based their possession of such power upon positive law, and not upon the doctrine of *self-*preservation, or legal necessity, is shown from the context; for he immediately adds that "though a very learned author" (Gilbert, Hist. C. P. Ch. 3) "seems inclinable to derive the process from the Statute of Westminster 2, 13 Edw. I, c. 39, * * * yet he afterwards more justly concludes, that it is a part of the *law of the land*, and, as such, is confirmed by the Statute of Magna Charta." 4 Bl. 286.

All that Blackstone absolutely knew of this power, and all that can be known of it, is, that from ancient times it was, by the law of the land, a power of certain courts in England. How it came to be so, is a matter of argument, not of authority. Nevertheless the opinion of the great Commentator is entitled to the very highest consideration, and it plainly stands against the pretension that the power of each of those courts to punish any contempt offered to it, accrued as part of the mere right of self-protection, and without the help of any specific grant.

If we turn to the history of the power, and consider the line which separated the courts which did, from those which did not possess it, we shall find the clearest indications that it was regarded as a question of jurisdiction, just as the other subjects on which the courts might respectively act were so regarded.

In the first place, we know that power to punish officers charged with the administration of the law under their control, and to punish contempts committed by any persons in their presence, was vested in the Sheriff's torn, in courts-leet, and in the coroner's court; Hawkins P. C., b. 2, c. 1, Sec. 14; c. 9, Sec. 41; c. 10, Secs. 1, 17; c. 11, Sec. 1. *Griesly's case*, 8 Coke, 38; *Garnett* vs. *Ferand*, 6 Barn. & Cress., 625; 3 Bl. 35; that it was not vested in courts-baron, hundred-courts, or county-courts, 3 Bl., 25, 33–35; and that the former were courts of record, while the latter were courts not of record. 4 Bl., 273; Hawkins, b. 2, c. 10, Sec. 1; c. 11, Sec. 1; 3 Bl., 33–35.

Now this discrimination cannot have been made on account of the inferior importance and dignity of the latter; for they were very ancient and absolutely indispensable parts of the general system of judicial justice; and in those times "the county court was a court of great dignity and splendour; the bishop and the ealderman (or earl), with the principal men of the shire, sitting therein to administer justice both in lay and ecclesiastical causes." 3 Bl., 36. Nor is it a sufficient explanation to say that, as fines and commitments must go of record, they could not be awarded by courts which had no record; for the real question is, why should not the county-court have been a court of record, at least for the purposes of this power? The distinction lay deeper; and was expressed in the fact that the courts of record were "*the King's* courts, in right of his crown and royal dignity," 3 Bl., 24; even a court-leet "being a King's Court, granted by charter to the lords of hundreds or manors," 4 Bl., 273; while the freeholders of the county, in right of their freeholds, were the real judges of the county-court, the Sheriff being only its ministerial officer, 3 Bl., 36; so that, like a court-baron or hundred-court, it was a court of *private men*. 3 Bl., 25. Equally with the court of the Sheriff in his torn, it was established by the law of the land, and, as it acted by the consent of the King, at least in the theory of the King himself and of the lawyers, it might be said to derive its powers from the crown, 3 Bl., 24; nevertheless it differed radically from the courts of record in this, that the latter, being the King's courts, and receiving their commissions and powers from him, either immediately or by charter, represented directly *the judicial power of the crown*, which could not be said of the county-court; since that tribunal acted by his consent merely, and was a court of private persons. This leads at once to a conclusion touching the very nature of contempts, and of the power employed in punishing them. They were not regarded as merely obstructions of the particular functionary charged with the administration of justice; they were offences *against the judicial power of the King;* and therefore it was the special business of the King's courts to punish and repress them; just as it was of their jurisdiction to take cognizance of all other offences against the King. (*a*)

Thus it appears that the very fact, that only those common law courts which were courts of record could fine or commit for contempts, is proof that the power was one of jurisdiction, and not a power accruing from the right of self-preservation. (*b*)

That this is the true character of the power, is recognized, in the distinctest manner, by the older writers on this subject. In *Griesley's* case, 8 Coke, 38, it appears that one Kingston was chosen constable by the jurors and presenters of a leet-court, and that *being present in the court*, he was charged by the Steward to take the oath, "which he utterly refused to do, and departed in contempt of the Court;"

(*a*) In an anonymous case, Willes, 459, it was held that a contempt of court was a *breach of the peace.* In *New Orleans* vs. *Steamship Company*, 20 Wallace, 387, Mr. Justice Swayne said: "Contempt of court is *a specific criminal offence.* The imposition of a fine was a judgment in a criminal case."

(*b*) 3 Steph. Com: on Laws of England: "All courts of record are courts of the sovereign, in right of the crown and royal dignity; and *therefore* every court of record has an authority to fine and imprison for contempt of its authority. * * * But the common-law courts not of record are of inferior dignity, and in a less proper sense the King's courts; and these are not *intrusted* with any power to fine and imprison the subjects of the realm, unless by express permission of some act of Parliament." And Blackstone, B. 3, p. 24, says: "All courts of record are the King's Courts, * * and *therefore* no other court hath authority to fine and imprison. * * A court not of record is the court of a private man; whom the law will not intrust with any discretionary power over the fortune or liberty of his fellow subjects."

whereupon he was fined one hundred solidi by the Steward. And because the said fine was not paid, the defendants, bailiffs, &c., distrained his cattle. Kingston now brought his replevin. The first question was, "whether the Steward might impose a fine in this case." The whole discussion turned upon the question, whether the judge must confine himself to an award of judgment generally, that the offender was *in misericordia domini regis;* leaving the amercement, as in cases of indictment, to be affered or taxed by the afferors; or might himself proceed at once to settle the sum to be paid for the default. Coke, mingling his own learning, in his usual manner, with the arguments of the case, puts the principle in the following passage: "There are two manner of offences, some done out of court, and some done in court; of those which are done out of court, the jurors of the leet have conusance, and therefore power to present them; but for contempts and misdemeanors in court, before the Steward himself, *he* hath conusance of them, and therefore may impose a fine for them, and thereof need not make inquiry; *so that those who have conusance of the thing are fit to impose a fine or amercement for the same thing.*" And Sergeant Hawkins, b. 2, c. 10, Sec. 19, says: "But if the amercement be for a contempt of the court, it may be settled by the judge himself, and needs no other afferement; for the judge of every court of record is *the most proper judge* of all contempts offered to such court; and *an amercement of this kind* is in the nature of a fine, and is so called in some books." And in another place, he says: "If the contempt happen to be done by a person present in the court, and it appears either from the confession of the person, or on his examination upon oath, or by the view or immediate observation of the judges themselves, *the court may immediately record the crime*, and commit the offender, and also inflict such punishment as shall seem proper."

We gather from these statements of Coke and Hawkins, that punishment of contempts was simply the administration of criminal justice, and had nothing whatever to do with self-protection. The only question was, who should have conusance of the offence; and the common law determined that the judge was the proper person; in a matter which occurred in his view or immediate observation, or which was ascertained by the confession of the person, or by his examination upon oath.

Finally, the pretension that this power originally accrued to the courts of record *ex necessitate*, and that it differed, in this respect, from their other jurisdictional powers, is completely refuted by the distinction made between superior and inferior courts of record in matters of contempt. The former were authorized to punish contempts generally, whether committed in court or elsewhere; the latter could punish only those contempts which were committed in court. In other words, the higher courts of record had jurisdiction to punish summarily such as might indirectly impede the judicial power, as well as those which immediately and directly obstructed it; while the lower courts of record could punish only direct obstructions. This distinction was even more significant than that between courts of record and courts not of record. It was one which necessity could not establish; it could only be the work of positive law, and could only happen in the process of distributing jurisdictional powers.

This matter was discussed in *Queen* vs. *Lefroy*, L. R. 8 Q. B., 134, where the question related to the power of the county courts established by statute. Mr. Justice Mellor said: "In 2 Hawkins, P. C. b. 2, c. 3, it is said the old jurisdiction of the one supreme court was introduced after the conquest, in which the grand justiciary acted as viceroy; and out of this court was erected the courts of Queen's Bench, Common Pleas and Exchequer; and therefore the foundation of the authority of these courts, as to contempts committed in court, and contempts committed out of court having a tendency to affect the administration of justice, was, that they were part of the great court or *aula regis*. The authority of the inferior courts of record has no such foundation; the matter stands on quite a different footing as to them; and no instance has been found where this power has been assumed or justified by any decision, otherwise than for contempts committed in face of the courts." The last words refer to the power of the inferior courts of record.

In the same case, Mr. Justice Quain said: "No authority is to be found for the existence of any such powers in an inferior court of record. The Superior Courts have always had the power of proceeding for contempts not committed in court. They had it, as Chief Justice Wilmot points out, by *immemorial usage*." Wilmot's Opin., 254. He adds that it was *not thought proper to intrust* such power to the inferior courts of record.

The power of courts of record to punish for contempts could not be placed more distinctly on the ground of jurisdiction vested by positive law, than it is in these opinions. According to one of the learned judges, the larger jurisdiction of the Superior Courts of Record belonged to them as parts of the *aula regis*, the King's own Court; and according to the other, by immemorial usage. It was also as King's Courts that the inferior courts of record exercised the more restricted power, but the King restricted them to that narrower jurisdiction, because it was not convenient that they should exercise the larger.

A recent case, decided in 1835, shows still more plainly that the English Courts, instead of deriving the power from necessity, as a remedy of self-protection, base it upon actual grant. In the *King* vs. *Faulkner*, 2 Cromp. Mees. & Rosc., 525, the power was denied because the grant was not clear. The act of 1 and 2 Wm. 4, c. 56, had created a Court of Bankruptcy, consisting of four judges and six commissioners, who, however, were not intended to meet as one tribunal. They were divided into several branches, one of which, composed of four judges, constituted a Court of Review; while each of the others, composed of three Commissioners, constituted a Court of Sub-division. These commisioners were also authorized to act singly.

A question, whether a Commissioner, sitting separately, had power to commit for contempt, arose under the first clause of the statute, which provided that "the same court shall be and constitute a court of law and equity, and shall, together with every judge and commissioner thereof, have, use, and exercise all the rights, incidents, and privileges of a court of record, * * as fully, to all intents and purposes, as the same are used, exercised and enjoyed by any of his Majesty's Courts of law, or Judges at Westminster." There can be no doubt that one of the "incidents" of a court of record, when that term is used broadly, was to commit for contempt; and if the words of this clause were to be accepted in that sense, a single commissioner would clearly be authorized by them so to commit. But, instead of seizing upon an opportunity to attribute this power, the Court of Exchequer explained away the literal force of the provision, and denied the power.

Chief Baron Abinger said: "I think so important a power, which requires the greatest nicety in its exercise, should not be vested merely *by an inferential construction* of an Act of Parliament, because in a general clause it invests him with the character of a judge of record. It is sufficient to say, if we are bound to find a meaning for every word in that clause, that the incidents and rights given to the judges of record were meant to protect him from being liable to the consequences of an action for any act he might do in the exercise of his functions; but it would not follow from that, that the legislature intended to give him all the powers of a Judge of a Court of Record to the full extent." And Alderson, B., said: "It seems to me that the first clause may have a very reasonable construction, without giving to the commissioner sitting alone the power contended for on the present occasion. * * * If you take the words to the letter, it would give to every commissioner the power and privilege of a court of record, as fully as they are exercised at Westminster. *I think it would require very strong words to induce the court to come to that conclusion.* The words of the Act may have a very sensible construction by being construed distributively; that is to say, by giving to *Courts* of Bankruptcy the incidents and privileges of a court of record, and by giving to the *judges and commissioners* of courts of bankruptcy the rights, incidents and privileges that belong to a judge of a court of record. No one of the rights, privileges and incidents of a Judge of a Court of record necessarily carries with it the power of committing for contempt; and therefore, it seems to me, that the first clause, by being construed distributively, may have a perfectly sensible construction, being intended to constitute *the Court* as a court of record, with all its rights, incidents and privileges; that is, having its records treated as all other records of another court, and each of its judges having the same protection and privileges which judges of the courts of record have, of not being answerable, in the shape of actions, for any acts which they have done in their judicial capacity and character. That will give a clear and sensible construction, *without giving this irresponsible power.*"

It may be remarked just here, that the court had in hand the construction of a *grant*, just as we have, in the question before us. In that case, however, it was plain that, taken literally, the words of the grant would give the power; while not a word descriptive of such a power appears in the Constitution of the United States; and the power itself must be an implication. Instead of having to consider whether they might graft anything upon the grant by implication, they had to consider whether they might not take something from it by construction; and Baron Alderson remarked that it would "require very strong words" to induce the court to conclude that the power was granted.

If the spirit of the courts of common law, in determining whether this peculiarly judicial power was conferred upon a judicial person, were applied in determining whether it has been conferred, by implication, upon legislative functionaries, there never would be an implication that it was conveyed by a grant of mere legislative power.

The special purpose, however, for which *Rex* vs. *Faulkner* is now cited, is to show that the English Courts have steadily, from the beginning down to the present time, held, that the English common law has never placed the power of judicial bodies to punish contempts, on the ground of inherent necessity, or on the principle of self-protection; but that they have always placed it upon positive grant, and have been very strict in construing the grant.

Let us turn from the history of this power of the courts in England, to what has been done in the same matter in our own country. It will appear by our legislation, that we have determined that this power is not inherent in the very constitution of a superior court; and that the possession and extent of it have been treated as a question of polity and convenience.

The Judiciary Act authorized the Courts of the United States " to punish, by fine and imprisonment, at the discretion of said courts, all contempts of authority in any cause or hearing before the same." In consequence of certain decisions, by which this provision was held to include the full measure of the common law power, Congress limited the authority of the courts by a rule of construction. The act of 2

March, 1831 (4 Stat. 487) provided: "that the power of the several courts of the United States to issue attachments and inflict summary punishments for contempts of court, shall not be construed to extend to any cases except the misbehavior of any person or persons in the presence of said courts, or so near thereto as to obstruct the administration of justice, the misbehavior of any of the officers of said courts in their official transactions, and the disobedience or resistance by any officer of the said courts, party, juror, witness or any other person or persons, to any lawful writ, process, order, rule, decree or command of the said courts."

This statute cuts off a large part of the power vested by the common law in the English superior courts of record; indeed almost all that distinguished them from the inferior courts of record. For example, the courts of the United States cannot punish, as a contempt, the offer of a bribe to the judge, or threats addressed to a witness, juror or party, not in its presence; or a libelous publication concerning pending proceedings. The common law held these acts to be obstructions of the administration of justice; but Congress has declared that power to punish them as contempts is not necessary to the courts of the United States. In other words, it has been declared that the functions of a superior court of record do not imply, as an incident necessary to the exercise of those functions, power to punish every act which obstructs them. For some of these obstructions, the same statute provides the ordinary and more deliberate remedy of indictment and trial by jury; but for others, such as libelous and contemptuous publications, tending to impede justice, no remedy at all is provided or permitted. However injurious they may be, it seems to have been deemed more important to avoid the risk of unduly restricting the liberty of the citizen, and especially the freedom of the press, than to protect the courts from such consequential obstructions as may be caused by abuse of that liberty.

The opinion of Congress, as to what protection is necessary to the administration of justice, is expressed in the second section of the Act of 1831, which provides: "That if any person or persons shall, corruptly, or by threats or force, endeavor to influence, intimidate, or impede any juror, witness, or officer in any court of the United States, in the discharge of his duty; or shall, corruptly, or by threats or force, obstruct or impede, or endeavor to obstruct or impede, the due administration of justice therein, every person or persons so offending shall be liable to prosecution therefor, by indictment, and shall, on conviction thereof, be punished by fine not exceeding five hundred dollars, or by imprisonment, not exceeding three months, or both, according to the nature and aggravation of the offence."

It appears, then, that, in dealing with this matter of contempts and obstructions, the legislature has decided, in the case of the courts at least, that immemorial usage had not established "the measure of necessity," nor indeed any necessity at all. It has been assumed that the whole matter belongs to the domain of polity, and is one of convenience.

In view of the fact that the claim of legislative power to punish contempts has been largely built upon what was declared to be the analogous necessity of such power to the courts, it is worth while to notice the bearing of these later conclusions upon some of the exercises of that power by Congress. Duane was imprisoned for defamation of the Senate, and Anderson for offering bribes to members of the House of Representatives. These offences were punished by those bodies, respectively, as *contempts;* and the pretension of power to inflict the punishment was supported by reference to the fact that such power belonged, *ex necessitate,* and on the principle of self-preservation, to every court of justice. It was claimed that it must exist in all analogous cases, and that the cases of legislative and judicial bodies were, in this respect, analogous. These two bodies, afterward, united in declaring, by the Act of 1831, that, in the example referred to, power to punish precisely similar obstructions did not exist, *ex necessitate.*

That statute, it should be remembered, was demanded of Congress by the common judgment of the country. Therefore, when that supreme tribunal decided that the power of summary punishment must be not only reduced, but very precisely defined before it should be entrusted, even, to functionaries who were designed wholly for judicial and deliberate action, equipped with appropriate methods, and protected, to a great degree, from passion and party feeling, by a life tenure of office; it is a fair implication that, on the principles of that judgment, a power without definition or limits is not fit to be exercised by bodies whose very function of making law tends to incapacitate them for a judicial application of law; who have not, and cannot have any sufficient means of perfect inquiry; who must inevitably be composed of the representatives of political parties, and who are beyond the reach of impeachment for an abuse of the power. By that statute, the country has effectively pronounced judgment against *all* pretensions to undefined and discretionary power over personal liberty, wherever they might be set up.

It is submitted that our examination of history and authority now justifies the following conclusions:

First. Power to punish contempts was acquired by the House of Commons and by the King's Courts by *grant*. It was granted to them by the common law; in other words by the British Constitution; just as the specified powers of our legislative and judicial departments have been granted by the Constitution of the United States.

Second. It was not granted on the ordinary principle of self-preservation, but because it was *proper and convenient* that they should have it, and as a power of jurisdiction.

Third. And, as a consequence or re-statement of these conclusions, the common law did not pretend to establish, and did not establish thereby, *any* conclusion as to what powers were necessarily incident to legislative assemblies and judicial bodies.

Fourth. When the question, what is necessarily incident to a legislative assembly, at last presented itself, the common law of England denied, as we have seen, that power to adjudicate and inflict punishment for contempts was incident to legislative assemblies, or was included in a common law grant of legislative power.

III.

If the foregoing conclusions be true, it is difficult to perceive how a reference to the common law can enable us to imply that this power is incident to the very existence of the two houses of Congress; since we should turn to that law only to learn that it denied the very proposition which we propose to establish.

But we propose now to show that, even if the common law had in fact held that such power was incident to legislative assemblies, that conclusion would be of no force whatever, in determining whether it belongs to the bodies established by our written Constitution. In other words, we propose to show that no reference to the common law, touching this matter, is authorized or permitted.

We are aware of the gravity of this undertaking. It is entered upon in face of a common assumption, for more than three-quarters of a century, that the common law, known as *lex parliamenti*, aids us in determining the "incidental powers" of these bodies, even where the Constitution contains no expression which refers to it. Commonly this assumption is only implied; but it is stated explicitly by the learned commentator on the Constitution. In speaking of the very power now in question, he says: "We may resort to the common law to aid us in interpreting such instruments and their powers; for that law is the common rule by which all our legislation is interpreted. It furnishes principles equally for civil and criminal justice, for public privileges and private rights. Now, by the common law, the power to punish contempts of this nature belongs *incidentally* to courts of justice and to each house of Parliament. No man ever doubted or denied its existence as to our colonial assemblies in general, whatever may have been thought as to particular exercises of it." Story, sec. 846.

It is immaterial to this part of our inquiry, that the hypothesis on which the learned author built his theory—namely, that power to punish contempts belonged "incidentally" to each house of Parliament—was itself unfounded, and has been swept away by the highest common law authorities. The question which we are now examining, is, whether, conceding it to be true that the common law held such power to be incident to legislative assemblies, any implication that similar power has been granted by our written Constitution to our legislative assemblies, can be based upon that fact. Has the common law anything to do with the matter?

It has never been questioned that, for purposes of "interpretation," in the proper sense of that word, we must often resort to the common law, in order to understand the Constitution. Provisions which employ its phraseology, necessarily refer the interpreter to the source from which they were borrowed, for an explanation. Not merely the verbal meaning, but the operation of a provision may be determined in this way. Familiar examples of this process, which have undergone judicial determination, are found in the provisions relating to the privilege of "the writ of habeas corpus," to the President's "power to grant pardons," to "due process of law," and to the right of trial by "jury." All of these are common law phrases understood to be used technically; therefore it is only from that law that we can learn what writ of habeas corpus it was, the privilege of which was not to be suspended except in certain cases; or how much was understood to be included in power to grant pardons; or what had been recognized as due process of law; or what was meant by a jury. The *principle* applied in these instances was perhaps still better illustrated by the provision which extended the judicial power of the United States to "all cases of admiralty and maritime jurisdiction." It was held in *Waring* v. *Clarke*, 5 Howard, 454, *et seq.*, that a collision occurring on tide-water was "a case of admiralty jurisdiction," notwithstanding it occurred also within the body of a county; and the same rule is now applied to cases happening above tide-water. When the Constitution was adopted, such a tort was understood *in this country* to be of admiralty jurisdiction, but was not so understood in England; and the Supreme Court held that these words had reference to the understanding here. In short, the general principle of interpretation has been, that the words of the Constitution may be explained by reference to the particular law from which they were borrowed, and that the Constitution itself intended to refer the interpreter to that source.

But in the matter under consideration, the Constitution cannot be said to have referred us to some other law in any such manner. It is alleged to have referred in *some way* to a power incident, by some other law, to legislative assemblies; but there is no pretence that it has done so by the use of any peculiar words or phrases touching legislative assemblies or legislative power. It simply provides that "*all legislative powers herein granted* shall be vested in a Congress of the United States, which shall consist of a Senate and a House of Representatives;" and afterwards grants those powers. The single intent of the provision in which legislative powers are mentioned, was to declare where those powers should belong, and that the body to which they belonged should consist of a Senate and a House of Representatives. It did not pretend to deal with the subject of legislative *power*, nor did it even characterize those bodies as legislative assemblies. It neither calls for nor admits of reference to external sources for explanation of its meaning. It establishes simply a *fact;* the fact, namely, that two bodies exist, and that those bodies are parts of a Congress which has certain legislative powers, and are themselves, therefore, actually legislative assemblies. The sole question, then, is whether this *fact* refers us to any other law for an implication of power known to be granted by that law.

The grounds of the argument which undertakes to work out this implication, are necessarily as follows: It is a *fact* that the authors of the Constitution established two legislative bodies; and it is a *fact* that the common law, recognized and adopted by them, gave to such bodies the power to punish contempts. Therefore they must have intended that these bodies should have the power which their common law gave to all such bodies.

This statement of the argument cannot be met by giving to it merely a new form; by saying, for example, that it must be supposed to have been the legal intent of the Constitution that the bodies which it established should have whatever powers its authors held to be necessary to the existence and safety of such bodies; and that their common law may be *referred to,* in order to ascertain what they did hold to be necessary.

This would only be to say, that, inasmuch as they had a common law, it must be supposed to have been their intent that it should operate, although not incorporated into the Constitution by a reference to it; and therefore that it should operate *as* their common law. If it was to operate when not referred to, the proposition comes at last to this: that, besides the Constitution, its authors had another law; and that when the written instrument gave existence to an institution, that other law gave it power. It is idle to talk about *reference* to the common law when none is made. Whatever effect that law should have, in such a case, must take place simply because it co-existed with the Constitution, and consequently by its own authority. We are reduced to suppose that the framers and adopters of the Constitution meant to do part of their work by written compact and part of it by their unwritten common law.

That the common law should clothe with power an institution to which it gave existence, is familiar enough doctrine; but that it cannot perform that office for a creature of legislation, has been settled by a line of decisions which cannot be shaken. It is the settled doctrine, in reference to the *courts* of the United States, that they may exercise common law powers only when the Constitution or the laws have made them constitutional or statutory powers; and that they cannot look to the common law as a *source* of jurisdiction.

The principle of that class of decisions is, that the common law regulates the powers of institutions created by our written law, only just so far as the written law, by some phrase of adoption, applies it to that institution; and this principle applies as perfectly to the legislative and executive as to the judicial institutions of this country. It is not our present business to deal with the question, Whether the common law of a *State* can clothe its legislative assemblies with this power, unless it is thus incorporated by the State Constitution; but it may be added, that the same reasoning which forbids the operation of common law, in the case of the legislative assemblies of the United States, would forbid its application in a like case to those of the States.

This assumption, that the authors and adopters of the Constitution intended that a common law power should attach, incidentally, to the new legislative assemblies, should rest on clear affirmative evidence that such an intention was universal; since the Constitution was not to be imposed upon all of the members of the old Confederation by a vote of the majority; and certainly no such assumption can stand if there is evidence that the people of any State did *not* so intend when they accepted the Constitution. This negative evidence exists. The protest made by the General Assembly of Virginia, only twelve years after the people of that State had voted to adopt that instrument, must be regarded as, for this purpose, a cotemporaneous exposition of their intentions. On the 11th of January, 1800, the

General Assembly of Virginia sent to the senators from that State an instruction, and to the representatives a request: "To oppose the passing of any law founded on, or recognizing the principle lately advanced, 'that the common law of England is in force under the government of the United States;' *excepting from such opposition, such particular parts of the common law as may have a sanction from the Constitution, so far as they are necessarily comprehended in the technical phrases which express the powers delegated to the government;* and excepting, also, such other parts thereof as may be adopted by Congress, as necessary and proper in carrying into execution the powers expressly delegated." See 1 Tucker's Blackstone, App. 433.

This protest was directed specially against the doctrine that the Courts of the United States had jurisdiction to punish common law offences; but it applied equally to the pretension that the *lex parliamentaria*, with its code of undefined offences, had been adopted by implication. It expressed, of course, the sentiment of the people of Virginia, and it is not to be supposed that they took a different attitude on this question only twelve years before, when they voted upon the adoption of the Constitution. But Virginia was not the only exception which broke the line of common consent to an implied adoption of *lex parliamenti*. Massachusetts and New Hampshire cannot be supposed to have assented to such an adoption, when they had already cut down its proportions by their own constitutions.

It is submitted, then, that the common law cannot be referred to, and cannot have any effect whatever in determining whether the power to punish contempts is incident to the existence of the two houses of Congress; first, because on general principle, the written instrument necessarily excluded the operation of any other law upon the institutions which it established, except so far as it referred to and adopted that law by the use of some express term; and second, because there is clear evidence that, as a matter of fact, some of the authors of the Constitution acted upon an understanding that the common law was not to have any operation, except in cases of such express reference. (a)

(a) Mr. Duponceau has admirably described, in the Preface to his Dissertation on the Jurisdiction of the Courts of the United States, p. viii, et seq., the difference between the relations which the common law bore to political institutions in England and the colonies, and those which it bore to institutions established by the written Constitutions of the States.

"In England, the country from whence we have derived, not only our system of jurisprudence, but most of our civil and political institutions, there is a metaphysical being called *common law*, which originally was a code of feudal customs, similar to the coutumes which, until lately, governed the different provinces of the neighboring Kingdom of France, but which, by gradual steps, and by force of circumstances has become incorporated and in a manner identified not only with the national jurisprudence, but, under the name of Constitution, with the political government of the country. The King's prerogative and the rights of the subject are alike defined and limited by the common law. The various and often conflicting jurisdictions of the different tribunals in which justice is administered are also said to be derived from it, although in many instances, they are known to be founded on gradual and successive assumptions of power; but those having been established and consolidated by time, are now become common law. This *ens rationis* is a part of every civil and political institution, and everything connected with the government of the country is said to be a part of it. Thus the law of nations, the law-merchant, the marine law, the Constitution, and even the religion of the kingdom, are considered to be parts and parcels of the common law. It pervades everything and everything is interwoven with it. Its extent is unlimited, its bounds are unknown; it varies with the successions of ages, and takes its color from the spirit of the times, the learning of the age, and the temper and disposition of the judges. It has experi-

But if these objections could be removed, it is submitted that another remains which must be fatal.

---

enced great changes at different periods, and is destined to experience more. It is from its very nature, uncertain and fluctuating; while to vulgar eyes, it appears fixed and stationary. Under the Tudors and the first Stewarts, forced loans, ward-ships, purveyance, monopolies, legislation by royal proclamation, and even the Star Chamber and High Commission Courts, and slavery itself, under the name of villenage, were parts of the common law. At the revolution it shook off these unworthy fetters, and assumed the character of manly freedom for which it is now so eminently distinguished.

"Twelve Judges, who hold their offices during good behavior, are the oracles of this mystical science. In a monarchy like England, which has no written Constitution, but in which all the rights of the Sovereign, as well as the privileges of the people, are to be deduced from the common law, those Judges are an useful check against the encroachments of the Monarch or his Ministers; hence the common law and the judicial power are, in that country, almost objects of idolatrous worship. While the United States were colonies, they partook of this national feeling; the grievances which induced them to separate from the mother country were considered as violations of the common law, and, at the very moment when independence was declared, the common law was claimed by an unanimous voice as the *birthright* of American citizens; for it was then considered as synonymous to the British Constitution, with which their civil rights and political liberties were considered to be identified. In the discussion that arose between the colonies and Great Britain, the *Constitution* or the *common law*, which was the same thing, was appealed to in favor of the doctrines which the contending parties respectively maintained. It was, therefore, held by all in equal veneration, and by all cherished as their most precious inheritance.

"The revolution has produced a different state of things in this country. Our political institutions no longer depend on uncertain traditions, but on the more solid foundation of express, written compacts. The common law is only occasionally referred to for interpretation of passages of our textual Constitutions and the Statutes made in aid of them, which have been expressed in its well-known phraseology, *but there ends its political empire*. It is no longer to it that our constitutional authorities look for the *source* of their delegated powers, which are only to be found in the letter or spirit of the instruments by which they have been granted.

"The common law, therefore, is to be considered in the United States, in no other light *than that of a system of jurisprudence*, venerable indeed for its antiquity; valuable for the principles of freedom which it cherishes and inculcates, and justly dear to us for the benefits that we have received from it; but still, in the happier state to which the revolution has raised us, it is *a system of jurisprudence, and nothing more.*"

The proposition that this power is incident to our legislative assemblies, stands upon an assumption that the founders of the Constitution had a common law, which was common to them to the same extent and in the same manner with the Constitution itself; that is to say, that the law to be referred to was the *common law of the authors of the Constitution.*

Now it is submitted that no such common law existed. A general common law, pervading all of the States as *one rule*, while those States expressly declared themselves, in their Articles of Confederation, to be sovereign and independent, and therefore to have independent systems of law, is not conceivable. And certainly, common law in that sense would not come into existence by force of the fact—if it had been a fact—that the common law systems of the several States were alike.

It was practicable, indeed, when the people of the several States resolved to come into closer relations, that they should establish such a body of law by their Constitution; but they omitted to do so, and it is the settled doctrine that, to this day, no such common law exists. In *Wheaton* vs. *Peters*, 8 Peters, 658, the Supreme Court of the United States said: "It is clear that there can be no common law of the United States. The federal government is composed of twenty-four sovereign and independent States; each of which may have its local usages, customs and common law. There is no principle which pervades the Union, and has the authority of law, which is not embodied in the Constitution or laws of the Union." See, also, *United States* vs. *Worrall*, 2 Dallas, 393; *United States* vs. *Hudson*, 7 Cranch, 32; *United States* vs.

Coolidge, 1 Wheaton, 415; *Pennsylvania* vs. *Wheeling Bridge*, 13 Howard, 563; *United States* vs. *New Bedford Bridge*, 1 Wood. & M., 435; *United States* vs. *Lancaster*, 2 McLean, 433; *United States* vs. *Wilson*, 2 Blatchf., 435.

The only remaining hypothesis is, that the authors of the Constitution acted with reference to the common law of the several States, and that they must be supposed to have intended that the two Houses of Congress should have whatever power those several unconnected bodies of law had declared to be incident to legislative assemblies.

Now, this implication assumes that the local laws of the States were coincident in this matter, and no such uniformity existed. The law on this subject, in Massachusetts and New Hampshire, differed from that of some of the other States and of England. Massachusetts, by her Constitution of 1780, and New Hampshire, by her Constitution of 1784, had restricted the power of their legislative assemblies to punish contempts, to narrower limits than those prescribed by the common law elsewhere. (*a*) What

---

(*a*) The Constitution of Massachusetts, adopted in 1780, contained the following provisions:

"X. The House of Representatives shall be the judge of the returns, elections, and qualifications of its own members, as pointed out in the constitution; shall choose their own Speaker; appoint their own officers, and settle the rules and orders of proceeding in their own House. They shall have authority to punish, by imprisonment, every person, not a member, who shall be guilty of disrespect to the House, by any disorderly, or contemptuous behavior, *in its presence; or who, in the town where the General Court is sitting and during the time of its sitting, shall threaten harm to the body or estate of any of its members*, for anything said or done in the House; or who shall *assault or arrest*, any witness, or other person, ordered to attend the House, in his way, in going or returning; or who shall rescue any person arrested by the order of the House.

becomes, then, of the supposed reference to the conclusions of the local laws of the several States, when this matter was regulated by the common law, in some of the States, and by written Constitutions in others; and when those conclusions, as to what power was necessary and incident to legislative assemblies,

---

"And no member of the House of Representatives shall be arrested, or held to bail, on mesne process, during his going unto, returning from, or his attending the General assembly.

" XI. The Senate shall have the same powers in the like cases; *and the Governor and Council shall have the same authority to punish in like cases;* provided that no imprisonment on the warrant or order of the Governor, Council, Senate, or House of Representatives, for either of the above-described offences, be for a term exceeding thirty days.

"And the Senate and House of Representatives may try, and determine all cases where their rights and privileges are concerned, and which, by the Constitution, they have authority to try and determine, by a committee of their own members, or in such other way as they may respectively think best."

The provisions of the Constitution of New Hampshire, of 1784, relating to this subject were as follows:

"The House of Representatives shall choose their own Speaker, appoint their own officers, and settle the rules of proceedings in their own House. They shall have authority to punish, by imprisonment, every person who shall be guilty of *disrespect to the House, in its presence,* by disorderly or contemptuous behavior, or by threatening or ill-treating any of its members; or by obstructing its deliberations; every person guilty of a breach of its privileges in making arrests for debt, or by assaulting any member during his attendance at any session; in assaulting or disturbing any one of its officers in the execution of any order or procedure of the House; in assaulting any witness, or other person ordered to attend by, or during his attendance of, the House; or in rescuing any person arrested by order of the House, knowing them to be such. The Senate, *President and Council* shall have the same powers in like cases, provided, that no imprisonment by either, for any offence, exceed ten days."

It is observable that the power to punish for contempt, specified in these two Constitutions, was extended to the Executives of those States, and that the causes for which such punishment might be inflicted, as well as the amount of the punishment, were much more limited than those allowed by the common law. Duane could not have been punished for his newspaper article under either of these provisions.

were not uniform? The base on which that implication of a grant of power is founded never existed, and the implication must fall.

Finally, if for want of uniformity, this implication cannot be founded upon the local laws of the States existing when the Constitution was framed and adopted, it would be to little purpose to show that this power had once been recognized by the common law in all the colonies. The question is, what was the common understanding at the time of the framing of the Constitution, not what it had been at some other time. The example of the colonies is, therefore, irrelevant, even if it could be shown that their rules, on this subject, were uniform.

IV.

Having considered whether the Constitution contains any *affirmative* implication of this power, we propose next to show that it contains *negative* implications—implications that it was not granted; and, further, that it contains provisions which actually prohibit the several houses of Congress to assume it.

It is plain—indeed the argument for the power stands on this ground—that the framers of the Constitution had carefully studied the privileges and powers of the two houses of Parliament; that they were aware of the privileges touching arrests and freedom of speech; of the right of the Commons to judge of the elections, returns, and qualifications of their members; to determine the rules of their proceedings; to punish and even expel their members; and punish persons who were not members, for contempt or breach of their privileges.

On the other hand, they must have known that the election of Speaker was still subject to the Crown's approval; that both Lords and Commons restricted the publication of their proceedings, so that even the votes of their members might remain unknown; and that both exercised the extraordinary power of compelling the assistance of every branch of the civil government in executing their warrants and orders. In short, they were familiar with parliamentary privilege, and knew how it had been used. What was their conduct under these circumstances, when they set about framing a new form of government, and what was its meaning?

Keeping these privileges and powers in view, and plainly copying from them, they proceeded to set down, in carefully limited terms, the privileges and powers of their own legislative assemblies. They provided that "senators and representatives * * shall in all cases, except treason, felony, and breach of the peace, be privileged from arrest during their attendance at the sessions of their respective houses, and in going to and returning from the same; and for any speech or debate in either house, they shall not be questioned in any other place;" that "the house of representatives shall chuse their speaker and other officers;" that "the senate shall chuse their other officers [than the Vice President] and also a President pro tempore, in the absence of the Vice President;" that "each house shall be judge of the elections, returns and qualifications of its own members;" that "each house may determine the rules of its proceedings, punish its members for disorderly behaviour, and, with the concurrence of two thirds, expel a member;" and that "each house shall keep a journal of its proceedings, and from time to time publish the same, excepting such part as may in their judgment require secrecy." They further provided a means by which the vote of each member might be known, by authorizing a demand of the yeas and nays; and, finally, they regulated the power of each house to make separate adjournments.

When we compare these details with the provisions of the *lex parliamentaria* and observe that some of the latter were adopted in the very language of that law, that some of them were restricted by new limits, that one of them was displaced by a contrary rule, and that some are not mentioned at all, it is impossible to doubt that the founders of the Constitution proposed to themselves to *select* from the common law those privileges and powers only, which should be suitable to their own legislative assemblies; or that they intentionally omitted, and intended to exclude, what they did not set down. The number and variety of the provisions which they took pains to make, would seem to be conclusive evidence that they intended to dispose of the whole subject of privilege and power; and it is a familiar rule of construction, that whatever is not contained in any document which undertakes to dispose of a whole subject, is rejected. The Supreme Court of the United States has even held, that any provision of an old statue which is not embodied in a new one which has this purpose, is *repealed;* although it may not be inconsistent with the provisions of the new act. Surely the same principle should apply, and with even greater force, to an original omission.

On the other hand, it is not supposable that the framers of the Constitution omitted to mention this power, because they thought that, being a power *ex necessitate*, it would take care of itself, without being mentioned; for power to expel a member is equally of that kind; and they were careful to specify that. We are not at liberty to presume that they acted on a theory which they did not observe. Moreover, such a supposition must assume that some, at least, of the delegates—for example, those from Massachusetts—were capable of trusting to implication, a matter which, in framing their State Constitution, they had deemed it necessary to provide for expressly.

In *Anderson* vs. *Dunn*, Mr. Justice Johnson sought

to dispose of the objection that *expressio unius exclusio est alterius*, by showing that an implication of constitutional powers, in disregard of that maxim, was familiar. He said: "There is an express grant of power to punish in one class of cases, and one only; and all the punishing power exercised by Congress in any cases, except those which relate to piracy and offences against the laws of nations, is derived from *implication*. Nor did the idea ever occur to any one, that an express grant, in one class of cases, repelled the assumption of the punishing power in any other."

We submit that the power of Congress to enact laws for the punishment of other offences than those specifically named, is *not* derived from implication. The general power "to make all laws which shall be necessary and proper for carrying into execution" the powers vested in Congress itself, or in the whole Government, or in any department or officer thereof, is just as much *an express grant of power* which covers crime, not specified, as the clause referred to is an express grant of power over the crimes therein specified. Powers which come within the description or operation of an express grant, stand themselves on the footing of expressly granted powers, notwithstanding they are not specified. If a law which provides punishment for a certain act, is a law which is necessary and proper for carrying into execution a certain constitutional power, then the power to make that law is expressly given. It is not *implied*, it is *ascertained* by determining that the particular law is one of the class described. This criticism is not new, nor unsupported by authority. In the *Legal Tender Cases*, 12 Wallace, 550, Mr. Justice Strong said: "We are accustomed to speak, for mere convenience, of the express and implied powers conferred upon Congress. But, in fact, the auxiliary powers, those necessary and appropriate to the execution of the other powers, singly described, are as expressly given as the power to declare war, or to establish uniform laws on the subject of bankruptcy. They are not catalogued, no list of them is made, but they are *grouped* in the last clause of Section 8, of the first article, and *granted in the same words* in which all other powers are granted to Congress."

It appears, then, that the examples referred to in *Anderson's* case, not being instances of implied power at all, do not even tend to show that when some powers have been granted expressly, others, which were not expressed, either specifically or generally, have been implied. But even if these examples had been instances of implied power, they would not have tended to prove that a power, not expressed, may yet be implied, if it appears that the expressed powers were intended to dispose of the whole subject of the powers to be granted. There is no reasonable pretence, (though such a pretence has been set up by too strict constructionists,) that the laws specified in the Constitution were intended to dispose of the whole subject of criminal legislation; while it is borne upon the face of the enumeration of the powers and privileges of Congress, that it was the intention to dispose of the subject of powers and privileges.

And it may be added, that the legal presumption founded upon this familiar rule, is supported by the historical situation. The Constitution was regarded by its authors as a new departure in government; and it was established by populations which were excessively jealous of the concessions they were about to make. The amendments which they demanded, in the very act of adopting it, such as the prohibition of an established religion and of an oppressive quartering of troops, showed a temper that would not risk even misconstructions which were almost impossible; but meant that they should be quite impossible. Can it be doubted that it was the prevailing intention of a people who were moved by such a spirit, to state, either in specific or general terms, and within the four corners of the written instrument, just what powers they were willing to grant to each department of this Government? Can it be supposed that they were willing to leave to implication what it was so easy to say, and what had been said in other constitutions? The principle laid down in *Marbury* v. *Madison*, 1 Cranch. 137, is almost a direct answer to such a question; for it was stated, not merely by a judge who had studied the Constitution, but by a man who personally knew its authors, that "The powers of the legislature are defined and limited; and that those limits may not be mistaken or forgotten, the Constitution is written. To what purpose are powers limited, and to what purpose is that limitation committed to writing, if these limits may, at any time, be passed by those intended to be restrained?" In the spirit of this rule we may ask: To what purpose were the independent powers of the several branches of the legislature committed to writing, if we may look beyond that writing, and search for new powers in the undefined and disputed common law of privilege?

To these considerations history adds another, which

bears directly upon the matter in hand. It was extremely improbable that the people of the American States should be willing to entrust this extraordinary and undefined power to their untried government. They were as well aware of its abuse by the House of Commons as of its existence, and they knew its natural tendency to extravagance. They knew that it had been the doctrine of that house, that whatever it claimed as a privilege became thereby a privilege. The judicial decisions which broke down that high pretension had not yet been made, and they had no certain ground for presuming that it would not be repeated here, if the law which permitted it should be adopted.

So far from having already grown more moderate, this theory was declared by the House of Commons itself fifty years later. Lord Denman said, in *Stockdale* v. *Hansard,* 9 Adol. & Ell. 108, (1839) : " If the Attorney General was right in contending, as he did more than once in express terms, that the House of Commons, by claiming anything as its privilege, thereby makes it a matter of privilege, and also that its own decision upon its own claim is binding and conclusive, then plainly this court cannot proceed in any inquiry into the matter, and has nothing to do but declare the claim well founded because it was made. This is the form in which I understand the committee of a late House of Commons to have asserted the privileges of both houses of parliament, and we are informed that a large majority of that House adopted the assertion."

But if the people of these States had no reason to apprehend new pretensions of privilege, it was enough to know how far they had already been carried. They were aware, for example, that the House of Commons, assuming to define what was a libel, had, in times of political excitement, punished as libels publications which questioned its powers, and that one Parliament punished such offences offered to another Parliament; that, from time to time, throughout the century preceding our Revolution, such acts as entering upon the estates of members, distraining their goods, lopping their trees, killing their rabbits, or fishing in their ponds had been punished as breaches of privilege. It is immaterial that these were only instances of usurpation and not of *lex parliamentaria;* for whether regarded as within or beyond that law, they would have the same effect in determining the disposition of our people toward that law itself—and it is of their disposition to import and adopt it, that we are speaking. But, as a matter of fact, they had no means of knowing what pretensions were legal and what were illegal; for Englishmen had actually been deterred from testing them by appeals to the Courts of Justice. Such appeals had themselves been treated as breaches of privilege. In the language of Lord Denman, in the great case already referred to, "None could have commenced a suit of any kind for the purpose, without incurring the displeasure of the offended house, instantly enforced if it happened to be sitting, and visiting all who had been concerned. During the session, it must be remembered that privilege is more formidable than prerogative, which must avenge itself by indictment or information, involving the tedious process of the law; while privilege, with one voice, accuses, condemns, and executes. And the order to 'take him,' addressed to the sergeant-at-arms, may condemn the offender to persecution and ruin."

It is impossible to imagine that these astonishing results of a power which refused to be defined should be unknown to intelligent persons in this country, or that they had been forgotten. Some of the most monstrous instances of its assertion, such as the noted case of Admiral Griffin's fishery, had occurred only a few years before our own contest with Parliament began. It could not fail to be fresh in the minds of all communities which had been subject to the power of that body, that Parliament had been made almost odious, certainly unpopular, among Englishmen themselves, by its use of privilege. Is it probable, then, that the people of these States, smarting under their recollections of wrongs, and submitting themselves only with hesitation and jealousy to any new control, could have intended silently to open the door, or rather to leave it ajar, for the admission of a power so indefinite, so capable of abuse, and known to have been abused and to have become odious in its original home? Did they bestow powers upon these untried legislative assemblies with such tokens of confidence, that we must infer from their very silence that they consented to be imprisoned by them, in any case where these bodies might conceive their dignity to have been assailed? Mr. Justice Johnson said in *Anderson's* case, "that the exercise of the powers given over their own members was of such a delicate nature, that a constitutional provision became necessary to communicate it. Constituted as that body is, of the delegates of confederated States, some such provision was necessary to guard against their mutual jealousy; since every proceeding against a representative would indirectly affect the honor or interests of the State which sent him." This particular reason did not apply to the private citizens of the States; but were those communities less jealous of the extent to which those citizens were to be subjected to the powers of the new government? We submit that their experience and their known sentiments suggest an extreme improbability that a power so undefined by law and so prone to extravagance, would be granted; and that the implications of History are as strong as the implications of the Constitution, that it was not granted.

Finally we come to the proposition that the Constitution contains provisions which actually forbid either house of Congress to assume the exercise of this power, as an original constitutional grant to it by implication.

By virtue of the general clause already referred to, the collective legislature has an express grant of power to make all laws which are necessary and proper for carrying into execution the powers and functions of *every* department and officer of this government, and among them the legislative power or function. For this purpose, it may not only provide punishments for all acts which obstruct the power or function in question, but may provide instrumentalities for their infliction. As a matter of fact, this power has, as we have already seen, been exercised for the protection of the legislative function, and of the effective working of the two Houses of Congress. The Act of 24 January, 1857 (11 St., 155), which provided for the punishment of recusant witnesses, summoned before either House, or before a Committee of either House, stood upon this ground alone. Its intent was to protect, not merely the legislative function, but the particular functions of each House; in other words, to afford precisely the kind of protection which is alleged to be the object and foundation of the power to punish for contempt. Now, if the collective legislature has control over this subject at all, it has such control in every case, and with regard to every form of obstruction, where the obstruction is offered by a person who is not a member. In the cases of members, the Constitution has vested in each House a power which is exclusive of legislative control; but, with this exception, the collective Congress has complete legislative control over the whole subject of offences which obstruct the functions or privileges of either of its branches. It may determine what acts shall constitute an obstruction or contempt, what penalties shall be inflicted upon the offender, and whether any particular kind of injury shall be punished at all. That this extent of power is vested in the whole Congress by an express grant of the Constitution, seems to have been conceded in *Anderson* vs. *Dunn*, although the learned justice who delivered the opinion conceived that an attempt to define the acts which should be punished, would be absurd.

Does not this express grant of power to the whole Congress make an end of the implication that the Constitution has granted to each House, independently, power over the same matter? If the Constitution has granted this power to each House directly, it must be an exclusive power, just as much as the power to judge of the elections, returns, and qualifications of its own members; to choose its own officers; and to determine its own rules of proceeding. And, surely, it is not necessary to demonstrate that an exclusive power in one House and a collective power in the whole Congress, are irreconcilable; or that, when the Constitution has expressly granted such power to one, we are not at liberty to *imply* that it has granted it to the other.

In the next place, this implication of a separate power in each House to punish contempts is forbidden, because the punishment of contempts was well understood, when the Constitution was framed, to be an exercise of *judicial power;* and the whole judicial power of the United States was disposed of by that instrument, without giving this portion of it to the several Houses of Congress.

What we mean by this proposition is, that it was known that the power of the House of Commons, in this matter, was a part of the judicial power of the realm, just as the jurisdictions of the common law, the Chancery, the Ecclesiastical, and the Admiralty Courts, were parts thereof; and that the House of Commons, in administering this portion of "the law of the land," acted in the capacity of a court, in as full a sense as those other tribunals were courts. We propose to examine the proofs of this statement.

In the first place, the adjudication of punishment for an offence is, in its very nature, a judicial act, a judicial judgment; and this is necessarily true, as well of the offence called a contempt, as of other offences. It was so regarded by the common law when the power to punish contempts was exercised by the Courts;

notwithstanding that proceeding has come to be spoken of as one of self-preservation; *Griesley's case,* 8 Coke, 38. In a word, it was a settled principle of the law of the land, long before this power and jurisdiction were vested in the House of Commons, that punishment of contempts by summary proceedings was an exercise of the judicial power, in the same sense and degree that punishment of other offences upon indictment was of that nature; and so clear was this principle, that it came to be held that, when power to punish for contempt was given to a body of persons, they were thereby erected into a judicial body. *Groenvelt* vs. *Burwell,* 1 Ld. Ray., 454; 1 Salk., 200. Is there any ground for imagining that the law, in granting to the Commons power to do the same act, attributed a different character to the power itself? The conclusion should be, on the contrary, that the nature of the power defined the capacity of its possessors, and erected them, to that extent, into a judicial body. That the grant of this power to the House of Commons was recognized to be a distribution of the judicial power of the realm, is conclusively established by the single fact that, from that time, all other tribunals were incapable of such jurisdiction. The jurisdiction of the Commons was necessarily regarded, and therefore was in fact regarded, as that of a higher court, and was not to be shared by the inferior courts. This was *essentially* a distribution of the judicial power of the realm; and the authorities show that it was held to be so in fact.

In the first place, the House of Commons itself assumed to act as a court. Evidence of this is found both in the style of its orders and in its express declarations. In 1586, when one White had arrested a member, it was ordered "that the Sergeant should warn White to be here to-morrow, *sitting the court.*" 1 Hatsell, 99. This language was used only forty-three years after *Ferrers' case;* the first in which power to try contempts was assumed. But they went further, and claimed to be technically a court of record. In 1592, when Thomas Fitzherbert, a member, was in execution, the matter was brought before the House by Sergeant Yelverton, and the question was, whether Fitzherbert should have the privilege. In the course of the debate it was resolved: "That this House, *being a court of record*, would take no notice of any matter of fact at all in the said case, but only of matter of record." 1 Hatsell, 107. And in the famous Apology of 1604, they said to James I: "We avouch also that our House is a court of record, and so ever esteemed." It seems they not only claimed that character as against the King, but restricted their own proceedings to the theory that they were a court of record.

This solicitude to be recognized, not merely as a court, but as technically a court of record, shows how distinctly the Commons themselves claimed that their power was judicial in the sense already known to the common law; and that, although limited, it was the same in kind with the judicial power exercised at Westminster Hall. It is impossible to mistake the sense in which they called themselves a court, when they were so careful to clothe themselves in the very fashions of judicial power. We know that the phrase was full of purpose. And they might well say that they had at least exercised the *powers* of a court of record before James's time. In sentencing Arthur Hall, in 1580, to a definite term of imprisonment and to the payment of a fine to the Queen, they had assumed precisely the functions of such a court. Indeed, so deadly earnest were they about the nature of their judicature, that they even attempted to exercise a general criminal jurisdiction. In 1621, when one Floyde, a catholic barrister, exulted over the mishaps of the Palatinate, they impeached him, as they called it, before their own house, and sentenced him to cruel punishments. In their debate they insisted that they had judicial criminal jurisdiction as much as the Lords, and could act alone. They gave way, it is true, when the Lords protested and the King asked them for precedents, and proceeded in the end by formal impeachment; but the very extravagance of their pretensions shows what they meant by judicial power.

But, however extravagant their pretensions may have been, their pretension to some extent of judicial power was universally accepted. The common-law courts and writers recognized their power in the matter of privilege to be judicial power in the exact sense to which they were accustomed.

In 4 Inst. 23, Coke said: "Now order doth require to treat of other matters of judicature in the lords' house, and of matters of judicature in the House of Commons. And it is to be known that the Lords in their house have power of judicature, and the Commons in their house have power of judicature, and both houses together have power of judicature." He then cites commitments for breach of privilege as examples of the judicature of the Commons. In other words, the jurisdiction of the Commons in the matter of privilege, and the judicial jurisdiction of the High Court of Parliament, which included both Houses, are classed together and described by the same word, and are thus alleged to be equally judicial power.

Sir Orlando Bridgeman, who was Chief Justice of the Court of Common Pleas in Charles II's time, was no friend of privilege, having been himself expelled by the Commons; but in the famous case of *Benyon* vs. *Evelyn*, while denying the particular privilege in question, he distinctly recognized that house as a court. He said: "I should have been glad not to have had occasion to have delivered my opinion on this point for two reasons; first, because it is a tender thing for an inferior court to judge of the privileges of a superior court," etc. Hargrave's MS. p. 6; Bridgeman's Rep. 324.

In 1704 the cases of the Aylesbury—men renewed with great heat the discussion of the capacity in which the Commons acted in committing for breach of privilege. It was clear enough that an action against a returning officer, for wrongfully and maliciously rejecting a vote, did not touch the privilege of the Commons to judge of the election itself; and nothing short of an inflexible rule could have prevented the courts from going behind the return to the writs of habeas corpus, and finding that the plaintiffs were imprisoned without having committed a contempt. But the rule was rigid and prevailed. In *Queen* vs. *Paty*, 2 Lord Raymond, 1109, 3 Anne, Mr. Justice Gould said: "If this had been a return of commitment by an inferior court, it had been naught, because it did not set out a sufficient cause of commitment; but this return being a commitment by the House of Commons, which is superior to this Court, it is not reversible for form." Mr. Justice Powys was more explicit. He said: "The House of Commons is a great court, and all things done by it are to be intended to have been *rite actæ*. * * The second objection was, that the warrant was not under seal, and 2 Ins., 52 is, that warrants of commitment must be in writing, under hand and seal. But to this I answer, that the House of Commons is a court, and so my Lord Coke says in his 4 Ins., 23; and commitments by a court need not be under hand and seal." It should be observed that this reasoning assumes that the House of Commons was a court in the most technical sense. Mr. Justice Powell dealt more philosophically with the matter, and explained that the Commons were a court to administer a separate branch of law, and were governed by the principles of that law. He said: "There is a *lex parliamenti;* for the common law is not the only law in this Kingdom; and the House of Commons do not commit by the common law, but by the law of Parliament. * * * The Commons have a power of judicature, and so is 4 Ins., 23; but that is not by the common law, but by the law of Parliament, to determine their own privileges; and it is by this law that these persons are committed. This Court may judge of privilege, but not contrary to the judgment of the House of Commons; which yet we must do in this case if we discharge these persons from their imprisonment; which is the only judgment the House of Commons can give upon their determination that these persons have been guilty of a breach of their privileges. * * * The Court of Parliament is a superior court to this court; and though the King's Bench have a power to prevent excesses in courts, yet they cannot prevent excesses in Parliament; because that is a superior court to them."

In 1751, Alexander Murray, being committed by the House of Commons for refusing to kneel at its bar, sued out a writ of habeas corpus; but the King's Bench refused to discharge him. In *Rex* vs. *Murray*, 1 Wilson, 299, Mr. Justice Wright said: "The House of Commons is undoubtedly a high court, and it is agreed on all hands that they have power to judge of their own privileges; it need not appear to us what the contempt was, for if it did appear, we could not judge thereof. * * * The House of Commons is superior to this court in this particular." And Foster, J. said: "The law of Parliament is part of the law of the land, and there would be an end of all law if the House of Commons could not commit for a contempt; all courts of record, even the lowest, may commit for contempt."

Twenty years later, the capacity in which the House of Commons acted in punishing contempts was stated still more emphatically in the famous case of *Brass Crosby*, 3 Wilson, 188. Lord Chief Justice De Grey said: "Lord Coke says they have a judicial power; each member has a judicial seat in the House; he speaks of matters of judicature of the House of Commons, 4 Ins., .23 * * * All contempts are either punishable in the court contemned, or in some higher court; now the Parliament has no superior court; therefore the contempts against either House can only be punished by themselves. * * * When the House of Commons adjudge anything to be a contempt, or a breach of privilege, their adjudication is a conviction, and their commitment, in consequence, is execution; and no court can discharge, or bail, a person that is in execution by the judgment of any other court. The House of Commons, therefore, having an authority to commit, and that commitment being an execution, the question is, what can this court do? It can do nothing when a person is in execution by the judgment of a court having a competent jurisdiction; in such a case this court is not a court of appeals." And, in referring to *Murray's* case, the learned Chief Justice said : "All the judges agreed that he must be remanded, because he was committed *by a court having competent jurisdiction.*" In the same case Gould, J., said: "They are the only judges of their own privileges; and that they may properly be called judges, appears, in 4 Ins., 47, where my Lord Coke says, an alien cannot be elected of the Parliament, because such a person can hold no place of judicature." Mr. Justice Blackstone was still more pointed. He said: "The House of Commons is a supreme court, and they are judges of their own privileges and contempts, more especially with respect to their own members: here is a member committed in execution by the judgment of his own House. All courts, *by which I mean to include the two Houses of Parliament and the courts of Westminster Hall,* can have no control in matters of contempt. The sole adjudication of contempts, and the punishment thereof, in any manner, belongs, exclusively and without interfering, to each respective court. Infinite confusion and disorder would follow, if courts could, by writ of habeas corpus, examine and determine the contempts of others. * * * No other court shall scan the judgment of a superior court, or the principal seat of justice; as I said before, it would occasion the utmost confusion if every court of this Hall should have power to examine the commitments of the other courts of the Hall for contempts; so that the judgment and commitment of each court, as to contempts, must be final and without control."

It is to be observed that, in all these opinions, the matter in hand was disposed of on the ground that not the slightest distinction could be made between the power exercised by the House of Commons and the power exercised by the courts of Westminster Hall. Even on the most technical points the same rule was held to be applicable to both bodies, because both were courts, administering, in an equal sense, judicial power.

It is a singular fact that Mr. Justice Story, who was of the opinion that the power to punish contempts was incident to legislative assemblies, should have cited *Brass Crosby's Case*, in order to show the conclusiveness of a commitment for contempt by an ordinary court of justice. In *Ex parte Kearney*, 7 Wheaton, 38, having laid down the proposition that, "When a court commits a party for a contempt, their adjudication is a conviction, and their commitment, in consequence, is execution," he added: "So the law was settled, upon full deliberation, in the case of *Brass Crosby*, Lord Mayor of London, 3 Wilson, 188. Indeed, in that case the same point was before the court as in this. It was an application to the Court of Common Pleas for an habeas corpus, to bring up the body of the Lord Mayor, who was committed for contempt by the House of Commons." The point under consideration was, the conclusiveness of a commitment for contempt by *a court*, and the learned judge assumed, that commitment by the House of Commons was an example of such commitment, and illustrated its conclusiveness.

It appears, then, that for two centuries before the adoption of our Constitution, it had been understood that the House of Commons exercised its power to punish contempts in the capacity of a court; and it appears by the same cases that it was understood to exercise a distributive share of the judicial power of the realm. When Mr. Justice Powell, delivering his opinion in *Paty's* case, said: "There is a *lex Parliamenti;* for the common law is not the only law in this kingdom; and the House of Commons do not commit men by the common law, but by the law of Parliament," and added that the Commons had "power of judicature * * * by the law of Parliament," he meant to explain that there was a distribution of judicial power, and that so much thereof as was of "common law" had been given to the courts at Westminster Hall, and that so much thereof as was *legis Parliamenti* had been given to the Houses of Parliament. This distribution of judicial power was effected by the British Constitution, and the House of Commons was held by that Constitution to be a court having competent jurisdiction to administer its share of the law. (*a*) It took this share to the

---

(*a*) In showing that the House of Commons was understood, when the Constitution of the United States was adopted, to be a Court, and to act in that capacity when it punished contempts, only decisions of a prior date have been cited in the text. Decisions of a later date are authoritative, however, to prove what the original theory was. Attention is, therefore

exclusion of all other courts, just as the Admiralty and Ecclesiastical and common law courts took their peculiar shares; and the whole of their jurisdictions, together, made up the judicial power of the realm.

With a full comprehension of this fact, the framers of our written Constitution undertook to make their distribution of judicial power. We will cite all of the provisions which can be supposed to touch that distribution.

---

called to some of them in this note. In the case of *Burdett* vs. *Abbott*, 14 East, 1 (1811), Lord Ellenborough used the following expressions: "Can the High Court of Parliament, or either of the two Houses, of which it consists, be deemed not to possess, intrinsically, the authority to punish summarily for contempts, which is acknowledged to belong, and is daily exercised as belonging, to every superior court of law, of less dignity, undoubtedly, than itself? * * * Upon this subject I will only say that if a commitment appeared to be for a *contempt* of the House of Commons, *generally*, I would neither, in the case of that Court or of any other of the superior courts, inquire further." In 1820, it was said in *Rex* vs. *Hobhouse*, 2 Chitty, 210: "The power of commitment for contempt is incident to every court of justice, and, more especially, it belongs to the High Court of Parliament." And, in 1847, Baron Parke, delivering the opinion of the Exchequer Chamber, in *Gossett* vs. *Howard*, 10 Adol. and Ell., 455, said: "The House of Commons is a part of the High Court of Parliament, which is, without question, not merely a superior but the supreme court in this country, and higher than the ordinary courts of law. Lord Camden, in *Entick* vs. *Carrington*, 10 How. St. Tr. 1047. And if we give credit to the courts of common law that they will not issue writs of attachment, except in due course and in accordance with the power which the law gives them, and that, notwithstanding the possible abuse of the liberty of the subject to which this principle may give rise by enabling the court to imprison for any cause, why should we not equally give credit to both branches of the High Court of Parliament that they, also, will duly execute their powers in obedience to the law from which they derive them, and to which, in common with all other courts, they are subject, though their course may also, possibly, lead to the same consequence, the abuse of the liberty of the subject, by their imprisoning any one at their mere will and pleasure?" In all of these cases the power of the House of Commons was sustained, not on the ground that it was analogous to that of the courts, but on the ground that it was, itself, a court.

The third section of Article 1 provides: "The Senate shall have the sole power to try all impeachments. When sitting for that purpose, they shall be on oath or affirmation. When the President of the United States is tried, the Chief Justice shall preside; and no person shall be convicted without the concurrence of two-thirds of the members present.

"Judgment in cases of impeachment shall not extend further than to removal from office, and disqualification to hold and enjoy any office of honor, trust or profit under the United States: but the party convicted shall nevertheless be liable and subject to indictment, trial, judgment and punishment according to law."

The fourth section of Article 2 provides: "The President, Vice-President and all civil officers of the United States, shall be removed from office on impeachment for, and conviction of, treason, bribery, or other high crimes and misdemeanors."

The fifth section of Article 1 provides: "Each house shall be the judge of the elections, returns and qualifications of its own members, and a majority of each shall constitute a quorum to do business; but a smaller number may adjourn from day to day, and may be authorized to compel the attendance of absent members, in such manner and under such penalties as each house may provide.

"Each house may * * punish its members for disorderly behavior, and, with the concurrence of two-thirds, expel a member."

The ninth section of Article 1 provides: "No bill of attainder * * shall be passed."

Article 3 provides: "The judicial power of the

United States shall be vested in one Supreme Court, and in such inferior courts as the Congress may from time to time ordain and establish. The Judges, both of the supreme and inferior courts, shall hold their offices during good behavior, and shall, at stated times, receive for their services a compensation which shall not be diminished during their continuance in office.

"The judicial power shall extend to all cases, in law and equity, arising under this Constitution, the laws of the United States, and treaties made, or which shall be made, under their authority; to all cases affecting ambassadors, other public ministers and consuls; to all cases of admiralty and maritime jurisdiction; to controversies to which the United States shall be a party; to controversies between two or more States; between a State and citizens of another State; between citizens of different States; between citizens of the same State claiming lands under grants of different States, and between a State, or the citizens thereof, and foreign States, citizens or subjects.

"In all cases affecting ambassadors, other public ministers and consuls, and those in which a State shall be a party, the Supreme Court shall have original jurisdiction. In all the other cases before mentioned, the Supreme Court shall have appellate jurisdiction, both as to law and fact, with such exceptions, and under such regulations as the Congress shall make.

"The trial of all crimes, except in cases of impeachment, shall be by jury; and such trial shall be held in the State where the said crimes shall have been committed; but when not committed within any State, the trial shall be at such place or places as the Congress may by law have directed."

The Amendments of the Constitution, relating to the exercise of judicial power, do not furnish any furher illustration of its distribution; but it is proper that they should be cited, in order that every provision touching that power may be presented. They are as follows :

"Article 4. The right of the people to be secure in their persons, houses, papers and effects against unreasonable searches and seizures, shall not be violated, and no warrant shall issue, but upon probable cause, supported by oath or affirmation, and particularly describing the place to be searched, and the persons or things to be seized."

" Article 5. No person shall be held to answer for a capital, or otherwise infamous crime, unless on a presentment or indictment of a grand jury, except in cases arising in the land or naval forces, or in the militia, when in actual service in time of war, or public danger; nor shall any person be subject for the same offence to be twice put in jeopardy of life or limb; nor shall be compelled, in any criminal case, to be a witness against himself, nor be deprived of life, liberty, or property, without due process of law; nor shall private property be taken for public use, without just compensation.

"Article 6. In all criminal prosecutions, the accused shall enjoy the right to a speedy and public trial; by an impartial jury of the State and district wherein the crime shall have been committed, which district shall have been previously ascertained by law, and to be informed of the nature and cause of the accusation; to be confronted with the witnesses against him; to have compulsory process for obtaining witnesses in his favor, and to have the assistance of counsel for his defense."

"Article 7. In suits at common law, where the value in controversy shall exceed twenty dollars, the right of trial by jury shall be preserved, and no fact tried by a jury shall be otherwise re-examined in any court of the United States, than according to the rules of the common law.

"Article 8. Excessive bail shall not be required, nor excessive fines imposed, nor cruel and unusual punishment inflicted."

These provisions of the original Constitution, and of the amendments made contemporaneously, suggest two considerations. First. It is impossible to read them without arriving at the conclusion that they contain all that the founders of this Government had to say, either of power that was technically judicial, or of power that was judicial in its nature and operation, and that they were intended to exhaust that subject. They vest certain judicial powers in the several branches of Congress, and certain other judicial powers in the courts of the United States. The provisions relating to the latter were manifestly intended to be exhaustive, and we have a right to suppose that the same intent prevailed in both cases. It follows that, on a principle which has already been explained, these elaborate affirmative provisions exclude an implication of any other judicial power, whether technically or effectually judicial. In other words, the power claimed for the two Houses of Congress, being judicial power, and not being mentioned in this exhaustive statement of the judicial powers distributed among the departments of the Government, must be denied on the principle of mere exclusion. The second consideration is, that a direct grant of this share of judicial power to the several branches of Congress cannot exist by implication, because the Constitution has *otherwise disposed of that very power*, by granting to another department a power which extends to and covers it. By authorizing the whole Congress to make laws providing punishment for contempts offered to either of its branches, and by extending "the judicial power of the United States" to all cases arising under such laws, the Constitution has authorized punishment of such offences *by the courts of the United States*. Now, inasmuch as a direct grant to each separate House, of jurisdiction over this class of offences, must be a grant of exclusive power, just as a grant of power to punish its own members for disorderly conduct is exclusive, such exclusive power and a power of the courts cannot co-exist. As the latter has been provided for expressly, the former inconsistent power cannot be implied. It is simply impossible that the Constitution should have intended to imply a power which was inconsistent with its own express provisions. In short, the power to punish contempts of either House of Congress has been *placed* by the Constitution, and there is no room for another claimant. They must be punished through the intervention of the "judicial power of the United States," vested in the Courts of the United States.

If this conclusion be well founded, another follows: no particular act can be punished as an offence against the authority or privileges of either House of Congress, until that act shall have been made an offence by statute. It has been settled that this Government has no unwritten criminal code, to which resort can be had as a source of jurisdiction. The courts of the United States must find the crimes which they undertake to punish, designated in the written law. *United States* vs. *Hudson,* 7 Cranch, 32 ; *United States* vs. *Coolidge,* 1 Wheaton, 415 ; *Pennsylvania* vs. *Wheeling Bridge,* 13 Howard, 519 ; *United States* vs. *Libby,* 1 Wood. & M., 222 ; *United States* vs. *New Bedford Bridge,* Ib. 401 ; *United States* vs. *Lancaster,* 2 McLean, 431. The only offences against Congress which have thus far been defined by statute, are bribery of members, Act 20 February, 1853, 10 Stat., 171 ; and the refusal of witnesses to testify when summoned before either House or before a committee of either House ; Act 24 January, 1857, 11 Stat., 155.

In conclusion, we revert to the emphatic declaration of Mr. Justice Johnston, in *Anderson* vs. *Dunn:* that this power, " if it exists, must be derived from implication " from the Constitution. It must stand as a power vested by that instrument directly in each House of Congress, on the same footing with its exclusive power to determine its own rules of proceedings, or it cannot stand at all. It is claimed that no such power has been granted. First. Because the Constitution contains no affirmative implication that it has been granted. Second. Because the Constitution contains implications that it has not been granted ; and, Third. Because the Constitution has not left this power dependent on implication, but has actually disposed of it in a manner which absolutely prohibits either House of Congress to exercise it ; having, by its express provisions, made punishment of contempts dependent wholly upon legislation, and applicable solely by " the judicial power of the United States."

If the conclusions reached in this inquiry be correct,

it does not follow that the privileges and dignity of the two houses of Congress should lose one jot of the protection which has hitherto surrounded them. That protection should, if possible, be even more effective than it has been; and the Constitution has furnished the means of making it so. The substitution of tribunals known to be unaffected by personal resentment, for a tribunal known to be affected by a sense of injured dignity and by party spirit; and the infliction of solemn punishment, defined and sanctioned by laws, in the stead of punishment prescribed by a law which is not known, and which has authority only by implication, would insure a common belief that the offence was grave, and that the punishment was just. A judicial conviction and sentence would accomplish what a commitment by order of either House has hitherto failed to accomplish; they would render the offence discreditable. And if it should be objected that judicial proceedings would, by reason of their slowness, impair the efficiency and defeat the objects of such punishment, it should be remembered that prompter methods may be contrived, without violating any provision of the Constitution. But even if this defect should prove to be, to some extent, permanent, it is still true that methods of administering criminal justice which are universally known to be authorized and trustworthy, are more useful than any method can be which is manifestly discordant with all our other constitutional habits, and which never fails to excite some apprehension touching its legality and fairness.

APPENDIX.

Anderson *vs.* Dunn.

6 *Wheaton*, 204.

Error to the Circuit Court of the District of Columbia.

This was an action of trespass, brought in the court below, by the plaintiff in error against the defendant in error, for an assault and battery and false imprisonment; to which the defendant pleaded the general issue, and a special plea of justification. The plaintiff demurred generally to the special plea, which was adjudged good, and the demurrer overruled; and judgment upon such demurrer was entered for the defendant, and a writ of error brought by the plaintiff. The question arising upon the demurrer will be best explained by giving the defendant's plea at large, as pleaded and adjudged good upon general demurrer in the Circuit Court, namely:

And the said Thomas, by the leave of the court here first had, further defends the force and injury, when, etc. And as to the coming with force and arms, or whatsoever is against the peace; and also as to the assaulting, beating, bruising, battering, and ill-treating of the said John, in manner and form as the said John, in his said declaration, hath above supposed to be done, the said Thomas saith that he is not guilty thereof; and of this he, as before, puts himself upon the country. And as to the imprisonment of the said John, and the keeping and detaining him in confinement, at the time in the said declaration mentioned, to wit, on the eighth day of January, in the year one thousand eight hundred and eighteen, and for the space of two months, in the said declaration mentioned, the said Thomas saith that the said John ought not to have or maintain his action aforesaid against him, because he saith that long before and at the said time when, etc., in the introduction of this plea mentioned, and during all the time in said declaration mentioned, a Congress of the United States was holden at Washington, in the county of Washington, and District of Columbia aforesaid, and was then and there, and during all the time aforesaid, assembled and sitting; and that long before and at the time when, etc., in the introduction of this plea mentioned, and during all the time in the said declaration mentioned, he, the said Thomas, was, and yet is, Sergeant-at-arms of the House of Representatives, (then and there being one of the Houses whereof the said Congress of the United States consisted,) and by virtue of his said office, and by the tenor and effect of the standing rules and orders ordained and established by the said House for determining of the rules of its proceedings, and by the force and effect of the laws and customs of the said House, and of the said Congress, was then and there, and during all the time aforesaid, and yet is duly authorized and required, amongst other things, to execute the commands of the said House, from time to time, together with all such process issued by authority thereof, as shall be directed to him by the Speaker of the said House; and that long before, and at the time when, etc., in the introduction of this plea mentioned, and during all the time in the declaration mentioned, one Henry Clay was, and yet is, the Speaker of the said House of Representatives, and by virtue of his said office, and by the tenor and effect of such standing rules and orders as aforesaid, and by the force and effect of such laws and customs as aforesaid, then and there, and during all the time aforesaid, was, and yet is, amongst other things, duly authorized and required to subscribe with his proper hand, and to seal with his seal, all writs, warrants and subpœnas issued by the order of the said House; and that long before and at the time when, etc., in the introduction of this plea mentioned, and during all the time in the said declaration mentioned, one Thomas Dougherty was, and yet is, the clerk of the said House of Representatives; and by virtue of his said office, and by the tenor and effect of such standing rules and orders as aforesaid, and by the force and effect of such laws and customs as aforesaid, then and there, and during all the time aforesaid, was, and yet is, amongst other things, duly authorized and required to attest and subscribe with his proper hand, all such writs, warrants and subpœnas issued by order of the said House; and that long before, and at the time when, etc., in the introduction of this plea mentioned, and during all the time in the said declaration mentioned, and ever since, it was, and yet is, amongst other things, ordained, established and practiced, by and under such standing rules and orders as aforesaid, and such laws and customs as aforesaid, that all writs, warrants, subpœnas, and other process issued by order of the said House, shall be under the hand and seal of the said Speaker of the said House, and attested by the said clerk of the said House; and, so being under the hand and seal of the said Speaker, and attested by the said clerk, as aforesaid, shall be executed pursuant to the tenor and effect of the same, by the said Sergeant-at-arms; and the said Thomas, the defendant, further saith that the said Henry Clay, so being such Speaker of the said House of Representatives as aforesaid, and the said Thomas Dougherty, so being such clerk of the same House as aforesaid, and he the said defendant, so being such Sergeant-at-arms of the same House as aforesaid, and the said Congress so being assembled and sitting as aforesaid, heretofore and before the said time when, etc., in the introduction of this plea mentioned, to wit, on the seventh day of January, in the year aforesaid, at Washington aforesaid, in the county and district aforesaid, it was, in and by the said House, *for good and sufficient cause to the same appearing*, resolved and ordered, pursuant to the tenor and effect of such standing rules and orders so ordained and established as aforesaid, and according to the force and effect of such laws and customs as aforesaid, *that the said John had been guilty of a breach of the privileges of the said House, and of a high contempt of the dignity and authority of the same; wherefore, it was then and there, in and by the said House, further resolved and ordered*, in the like pursuance of such standing rules and orders as aforesaid, and of such laws and customs as aforesaid, that the said Speaker should forthwith issue his warrant, directed to the Sergeant-at-arms, commanding him to take into custody the body of the said John, wherever to be found, and the same forthwith to have *before the said House, at the bar thereof, then and there to answer to the said charge,* etc., as by the journal, record and the proceedings of the said resolutions and order in the said House remaining, reference being thereto had, will more fully appear. Whereupon, the said Henry Clay, so being such Speaker as aforesaid, in pursuance of such standing rules and orders as aforesaid, and according to such laws and customs as aforesaid, did, *for the execution of the resolution and order aforesaid,* afterwards and before the time when, etc., in the introduction of this plea mentioned, to wit, on the seventh day of January, in the year aforesaid, at Washington aforesaid, in the county aforesaid, as such Speaker as aforesaid, duly make and issue his certain warrant, under his hand and seal, duly directed to the said Thomas, the defendant, as such Sergeant-at-arms, as aforesaid, (to whom, so being such Sergeant-at-arms as aforesaid, the execution of that warrant then and there belonged,) and by the said Thomas Dougherty, so being such clerk as aforesaid; in and by said warrant, *reciting that the said House of Representatives had, that day, resolved and adjudged that the said John Anderson had been guilty of a breach of the privileges of the said House, and of a high contempt of its dignity and authority;* and that the said House had thereupon ordered the Speaker to issue his warrant directed to the said Sergeant-at-arms, commanding him, the said Sergeant, to take into custody the body of the said John Anderson, wherever to be found, *and the same forthwith to have before the said House, at the bar thereof, then and there to answer to the said charge;* therefore, it was required that the said Thomas, the defendant, as such Sergeant as aforesaid,

should take into his custody the body of the said John
Anderson, and then forthwith to bring him before the
said House at the bar thereof, then and there *to answer
to the charge aforesaid, and to be dealt with by the said
House, according to the Constitution and laws of the
United States;* and the said Henry Clay, so being
such Speaker as aforesaid, then and there, and before
the said time when, etc., in the introduction of this
plea mentioned, delivered the said warrant to the said
Thomas, so being such Sergeant as aforesaid, to be
executed in due form of law. By virtue, and in execution of which said warrant, the said Thomas, as such
Sergeant as aforesaid, afterwards, to wit, at the same
time when, etc., in the introduction of this plea mentioned, at Washington aforesaid, in order to arrest the
said John, and convey him in custody to the bar of
the said House, to answer to the charge aforesaid, and
to be dealt with by the said House according to the
Constitution and laws of the United States, in obedience to the resolutions and order aforesaid, and to
the tenor and effect of the said warrant, so issued as
aforesaid, went to the said John, and then and there
gently laid his hands on the said John to arrest
him, and did then and there arrest him by his body,
and take him into custody, and did then forthwith
convey him to the bar of the said House, as it was lawful for the said Thomas to do for the cause aforesaid;
and thereupon such proceedings were had, in and by
the said House, that the said John was then and there
forthwith duly examined, and heard in his defense, before the said House, at the bar thereof, touching the
matter of the said charge; and that such examination
was, in and by the said House, and by the resolutions

and orders of the same, duly adjourned and continued from day to day, from the time when, etc., in the introduction of this plea mentioned, until the sixteenth day of January, in the year aforesaid; which said examinations were then so adjourned and continued, as aforesaid from necessity, in order to go through and conclude the examination and defence of the said John, touching the matter of the said charge, before the said House; neither the said examination, nor the said defense having been finished or concluded before the day last aforesaid; during all which time, to wit, from the said time when, etc., in the introduction of this plea mentioned, until the day last aforesaid, it was, in and by the said House, duly resolved and ordered, from day to day, as the said examination was adjourned and continued as aforesaid, that the said John should be remanded, kept, and detained in the custody of the said Thomas, as such Sergeant aforesaid, by virtue and in execution of the said warrant, in order to have such his examinations and defense finished and concluded in due form; and the said Thomas, as such Sergeant as aforesaid, afterwards, to wit, at and from the said time when, etc., in the introduction of this plea mentioned, until the said sixteenth day of January, in the year aforesaid, did, in pursuance of the last-mentioned resolutions and orders of said House, and by virtue, and in execution of the said warrant, keep and detain the said John in custody as aforesaid, and him did bring and have, from day to day, during the said time, before the said House, at the bar thereof, in order to undergo such examinations as aforesaid, and to be heard in his defense aforesaid, touching the matter of the said charge, to wit, at Washington aforesaid, in

the county aforesaid, as it was also lawful for him, the
said Thomas, to do for the cause aforesaid; and thereupon afterwards, to wit, on the said last-mentioned
sixteenth day of January, in the year aforesaid, such further proceedings were had in and by the said House
that it was then and there finally resolved and *adjudged
in and by the said House, that the said John was
guilty and convicted of the charge aforesaid, in the
form aforesaid;* and that he be forthwith brought to
the bar of the said House, and there reprimanded by
the said Speaker, for the outrage by the said John
committed, and then that he be forthwith discharged
from the custody of the said Sergeant-at-arms; and
thereupon the said John was then and there, in pursuance of the last-mentioned resolutions, order and
judgment, forthwith reprimanded by the said Speaker,
and then forthwith discharged from the arrest and
custody aforesaid; as by the journals, record and
proceedings of the said resolutions, orders, and judgment in the said House remaining, reference being
thereto had will more fully appear; which are the
same several supposed trespasses in the introduction
of this plea mentioned, and whereof the said John
hath, above in his said declaration, complained
against the said Thomas, and not other or different;
with this, that the said Thomas doth aver that the
said John, the now plaintiff, and the said John
Anderson, in the said resolutions, orders, warrants,
and judgment respectively mentioned, was, and is, one
and the same person; and that the said several times
in this plea mentioned, and during all the time
therein mentioned, the said Congress of the United
States was assembled and sitting, to wit, at Washing-

ton aforesaid, in the county aforesaid; and this the said Thomas is ready to verify; wherefore he prays judgment, if the said John ought to have or maintain his aforesaid action against him, etc.

JOHNSON, J., delivered the opinion of the court.

Notwithstanding the range which has been taken by the plaintiff's counsel, in the discussion of this cause, the merits of it really lie in a very limited compass. The pleadings have narrowed them down to the simple inquiry, whether the House of Representatives can take cognizance of contempts committed against themselves, under any circumstances? The duress complained of was sustained under a warrant issued to compel the party's appearance, not for the actual infliction of punishment for an offense committed. Yet it cannot be denied, that the power to institute a prosecution must be dependent upon the power to punish. If the House of Representative possessed no authority to punish for contempt, the initiating process issued in the assertion of that authority must have been illegal; there was a want of jurisdiction to justify it.

It is certainly true, that there is no power given by the Constitution to either House to punish for contempts, except when committed by their own members. Nor does the judicial or criminal power given to the United States, in any part, expressly extend to the infliction of punishment for contempt of either house, or any one coördinate branch of the government. Shall we, therefore, decide that no such power exists?(a)

(a) It is implied in this passage that the Constitution has omitted to extend the judicial power of the United States to the punishment of contempts of Congress, just as much as it has omitted to extend the power of the several houses to that subject; in other words, that they stand on the

It is true that such a power, if it exists, must be derived from implication, and the genius and spirit of our institutions are hostile to the exercise of implied powers. Had the faculties of man been competent to the framing of a system of government which would have left nothing to implication, it cannot be doubted that the effort would have been made by the framers of the Constitution. But what is the fact? There is not in the whole of that admirable instrument, a grant of powers which does not draw after it others, not expressed, but vital to their exercise; not substantive and independent, in deed, but auxiliary and subordinate.

The idea is utopian, that government can exist without leaving the exercise of discretion somewhere. Public security against the abuse of such discretion must rest on responsibility, and stated appeals to public approbation. Where all power is derived from the people, and public functionaries, at short intervals, deposit it at the feet of the people, to be resumed again only at their will, individual fears may be alarmed by the monsters of imagination, but individual liberty can be in little danger.

No one is so visionary as to dispute the assertion,

---

same footing as to any express provision which enables their power to reach the subject. Manifestly this is an error. The Constitution does not *specify* contempts of Congress, as a matter to which the judicial power extends; but it does expressly extend that power to the punishment of any act which Congress may constitutionally declare to be an offense. It is on the ground that it does so extend, that all existing crimes against the United States are punishable by the courts of the United States; and contempts of Congress are provided for in precisely the same manner with the whole body of crimes. There is therefore the broadest difference between the positions of the courts and of the two houses of Congress. The Constitution has expressly extended the power of the former to this subject, and is silent as to the latter.

that the sole end and aim of all our institutions is the safety and happiness of the citizen. But the relation between the action and the end, is not always so direct and palpable as to strike the eye of every observer. The science of government is the most abstruse of all sciences; if, indeed, that can be called a science which has but few fixed principles, and practically consists in little more than the exercise of a sound discretion, applied to the exigencies of the state as they arise. It is the science of experiment.

But if there is one maxim which necessarily rides over all others, in the practical application of government, it is, that the public functionaries must be left at liberty to exercise the powers which the people have intrusted to them. The interests and dignity of those who created them require the exertion of the powers indispensable to the attainment of the ends of their creation. Nor is a casual conflict with the rights of particular individuals any reason to be urged against the exercise of such powers. The wretch beneath the gallows may repine at the fate which awaits him, and yet it is no less certain that the laws under which he suffers were made for his security. The unreasonable murmurs of individuals against the restraints of society, have a direct tendency to produce that worst of all despotisms, which makes every individual the tyrant over his neighbor's rights.

That "the safety of the people is the supreme law," not only comports with, but is indispensable to, the exercise of those powers in their public functionaries, without which that safety cannot be guarded. On this principle it is, that courts of justice are universally acknowledged to be vested, by their very creation, with power to impose silence, respect, and decorum, in their presence, and submission to their lawful mandates, and, as a corollary to this proposition, to preserve themselves and their officers from the approach and insults of pollution.

It is true, that the courts of justice of the United States are vested, by express statute provision, with power to fine and imprison for contempts; but it does not follow, from this circumstance, that they would not have exercised that power without the aid of the statute, or not in cases, if such should occur, to which such statute provision may not extend; on the contrary, it is a legislative assertion of this right, as incident to a grant of judicial power, and can only be considered either as an instance of abundant caution, or a legislative declaration, that the power of punishing for contempt shall not extend beyond its known and acknowledged limits of fine and imprisonment.

But it is contended, that if this power in the House of Representatives is to be asserted on the plea of necessity, the ground is too broad, and the result too indefinite; that the executive, and every coördinate, and even subordinate branch of the government, may resort to the same justification, and the whole assume to themselves, in the exercise of this power, the most tyrannical licentiousness.

This is, unquestionably, an evil to be guarded against; and if the doctrine may be pushed to that extent, it must be a bad doctrine, and is justly denounced.

But what is the alternative? The argument obviously leads to the total annihilation of the power of the House of Representatives to guard itself from contempts, and leaves it exposed to every indignity and interruption that rudeness, caprice, or even conspiracy, may meditate against it. This result is fraught with too much absurdity not to bring into doubt the soundness of any argument from which it is derived. That a deliberative assembly, clothed with the majesty of the people, and charged with the care of all that is dear to them; composed of the most distinguished citizens, selected and drawn together from every quarter of a great nation; whose deliberations are required by public opinion to be conducted under the eye of the public, and whose decisions must be clothed with all that sanctity which unlimited confidence in their wisdom and purity can inspire; that such an assembly should not possess the power to suppress rudeness, or repel insult, is a supposition too wild to be suggested. And, accordingly, to avoid the pressure of these considerations, it has been argued that the right of the respective houses to exclude from their presence, and their absolute control within their own walls, carry with them the right to punish contempts committed in their presence;(a) while the absolute legislative power given to Congress, within this district, enables them to provide by law against all other insults against which there is any necessity for providing.

It is to be observed, that so far as the issue of this cause is implicated, this argument yields all right of the plaintiff in error to a decision in his favor; for *non constat*, from the pleadings, but that this warrant

---

(*a*) It is denied, in the present inquiry, that the absolute control of the respective houses within their own walls carries with it any such power in the case supposed.

issued for an offense committed in the immediate presence of the house.

Nor is it immaterial to notice what difficulties the negation of this right in the House of Representatives draws after it, when it is considered that the concession of the power, if exercised within their walls, relinquishes the great grounds of the argument, to wit: the want of an express grant, and the unrestricted and undefined nature of the power here set up. For why should the house be at liberty to exercise an ungranted, an unlimited, and undefined power within their walls, any more than without them? If the analogy with individual right and power be resorted to, it will reach no further than to exclusion, and it requires no exuberance of imagination to exhibit the ridiculous consequences which might result from such a restriction, imposed upon the conduct of a deliberative assembly.

Nor would their situation be materially relieved by resorting to their legislative power within the district. That power may, indeed, be applied to many purposes, and was intended by the Constitution to extend to many purposes indispensable to the security and dignity of the General Government; but they are purposes of a more grave and general character than the offenses which may be denominated contempts, and which, from their very nature, admit of no precise definition. Judicial gravity will not admit of the illustrations which this remark would admit of. Its correctness is easily tested by pursuing, in imagination, a legislative attempt at defining the cases to which the epithet contempt might be reasonably applied.

But although the offense be held undefinable, it is

justly contended that the punishment need not be indefinite. Nor is it so.

We are now considering the extent to which the punishing power of Congress, by a legislative act, may be carried. On that subject, the bounds of their power are to be found in the provisions of the Constitution.

The present question is, what is the extent of the *punishing power* which the deliberative assemblies of the Union may assume and exercise *on the principle of self-preservation?*

Analogy, and the nature of the case, furnish the answer: "The least power adequate to the end proposed;" which is the power of imprisonment. It may, at first view, and from the history of the practice of our legislative bodies, be thought to extend to other inflictions. But every other will be found to be mere commutation for confinement; since commitment alone is the alternative where the individual proves contumacious. And even to the duration of imprisonment a period is imposed by the nature of things, since the existence of the power that imprisons is indispensable to its continuance; and although the legislative power continues perpetual, the legislative body ceases to exist on the moment of its adjournment or periodical dissolution. It follows that imprisionment must terminate with that adjournment.

This view of the subject necessarily sets bounds to the exercise of a caprice which has sometimes disgraced deliberative assemblies, when under the influence of strong passions, or wicked leaders, but the instances of which have long since remained on record only as historical facts, not as precedents for initation. In the present fixed and settled state of English institutions, there is no more danger of their being revived, probably, than in our own.

But the American legislative bodies have never possessed, or pretended to the omnipotence which constitutes the leading feature in the legislative assembly of Great Britain, and which may have led occasionally to the exercise of caprice, under the specious appearance of merited resentment.

If it be inquired, what security is there, that with an officer avowing himself devoted to their will, the House of Representatives will confine its punishing power to the limits of imprisonment, and not push it to the infliction of corporal punishment, or even death, and exercise it in cases affecting the liberty of speech, and of the press? the reply is to be found in the consideration that the Constitution was formed in and for an advanced state of society, and rests at every point on received opinions and fixed ideas. It is not a new creation, but a combination of existing materials, whose properties and attributes were familiarly understood, and had been determined by reiterated experiments. It is not, therefore, reasoning upon things as they are, to suppose that any deliberative assembly, constituted under it, would ever assert any other rights and powers than those which had been established by long practice, and conceded by public opinion. Melancholy, also, would be that state of distrust which rests not a hope upon a moral influence. The most absolute tyranny could not subsist where men could not be trusted with power because they might abuse it, much less a government which has no other basis than the same morals, moderation, and good sense of those who compose it. Unreasonable jealousies not only blight the pleasures, but dissolve the very texture of society.

But it is argued that the inference, if any, arising under the Constitution, is against the exercise of the powers here asserted by the House of Representatives; that the express grant of power to punish their members respectively, and to expel them, by the application of a familiar maxim, raises an implication against the power to punish any other than their own members.

This argument proves too much; for its direct application would lead to the annihilation of almost every power of Congress. To enforce its laws upon any subject without the sanction of punishment is obviously impossible. Yet there is an express grant of power to punish in one class of cases, and one only; and all the punishing power exercised by Congress in any cases, except those which relate to piracy and offences against the laws of nations, is derived from implication.(a) Nor did the idea ever occur to any one, that the express grant in one class of cases repelled the assumption of the punishing power in any other.

The truth is, that the exercise of the powers given over their own members, was of such a delicate nature, that a constitutional provision became necessary to assert or communicate it. Constituted as that body is, of the delegates of confederated States, some such

---

(a) The power of Congress to enact penal laws which are necessary and proper for carrying into execution any power of this government, does not arise by implication. It is given in the same terms with all other powers of Congress. That is to say, it is given *expressly*. It is found in the last clause of section 8, Article 1. In using this express power, Congress is not called upon to imply anything; it has only to ascertain that the thing proposed comes within the descriptive terms, "necessary and proper," etc.

provision was necessary to guard against their mutual jealousy, since every proceeding against a representative would indirectly affect the honor or interests of the State which sent him.

In reply to the suggestion that, on this same foundation of necessity, might be raised a superstructure of implied powers in the executive, and every other department, and even ministerial officers of the government, it would be sufficient to observe, that neither analogy nor precedent would support the assertion of such powers in any other than a legislative or judicial body. Even corruption anywhere else would not contaminate the source of political life. In the retirement of the cabinet, it is not expected that the executive can be approached by indignity or insult; nor can it ever be necessary to the executive, or any other department, to hold a public deliberative assembly. These are not arguments; they are visions which mar the enjoyment of actual blessings with the attack or feint of the harpies of imagination.

As to the minor points made in this case, it is only necessary to observe, that there is nothing on the face of this record from which it can appear on what evidence this warrant was issued. And we are not to presume that the House of Representatives would have issued it without duly establishing the fact charged upon the individual. And, as to the distance to which the process might reach, it is very clear that there exists no reason for confining its operation to the limits of the District of Columbia; after passing these limits, we know no bounds that can be prescribed to its range but those of the United States. And why should it be restricted at other boundaries? Such are the limits of the legislating powers of that body; and the inhabitant of Louisiana or Maine may as probably charge them with bribery and corruption, or attempt, by letter, to induce the commission of either, as the inhabitant of any other section of the Union. If the inconvenience be urged, the reply is obvious; there is no difficulty in observing that respectful deportment which will render all apprehension chimerical.

Judgment affirmed.

www.ingramcontent.com/pod-product-compliance
Lightning Source LLC
Chambersburg PA
CBHW020312170426
43202CB00008B/582